M000206750

Peter L. Berger
The Many Altars of Modernity

Peter L. Berger

The Many Altars of Modernity

Toward a Paradigm for Religion in a Pluralist Age

DE GRUYTER

ISBN 978-1-61451-750-4
e-ISBN 978-1-61451-647-7

Library of Congress Cataloging-in-Publication Data
A CIP catalog record for this book has been applied for at the Library of Congress.

Bibliographic Information published by the Deutsche Nationalbibliothek
The Deutsche Nationalbibliothek lists this publication in the Deutsche Nationalbibliografie;
detailed bibliographic data are available on the Internet at http://dnb.dnb.de.

© 2014 Walter de Gruyter, Inc., Boston/Berlin
Printing and binding: CPI books GmbH, Leck
♾ Printed on acid-free paper
Printed in the USA by Edwards Brothers Malloy

www.degruyter.com

To Brigitte Berger, who has been listening to my obsessions about religion for many years – patiently, supportively, but by no means uncritically.

Contents

Contents

Preface

Secularization theory, based on the idea that modernity necessarily brings about a decline of religion, has for a time served as a paradigm for the study of religion. It can no longer be maintained in the face of the empirical evidence. A new paradigm is needed. I think that it must be based on the many implications of the phenomenon of pluralism. I propose that a new paradigm should be able to deal with two pluralisms – the co-existence of different religions and the co-existence of religious and secular discourses. This co-existence occurs both in the minds of individuals and in social space. I intend this book to be a step toward such a paradigm for the understanding of modernity and religion.

Having reached a truly intimidating age (it mainly intimidates me), I have been pleased to find that over the last two years or so I have had some genuinely new ideas about a topic that has occupied me throughout my career as a sociologist – namely, the relation of religion and modernity. Perhaps these ideas are false, but the fact that they are new is satisfying in itself – it seems that the drooling phase of my intellectual biography has not, or not yet, arrived!

In the early phase of my work in the sociology of religion I assumed the validity of what was then called secularization theory. Its basic idea was quite simple: Modernity necessarily brings about a decline of religion. I was not alone in this: The theory, in one formulation or another, was assumed by nearly everyone studying religion in the modern world – by children of the Enlightenment who welcomed the alleged fact of religious decline (even some theologians managed this attitude), and by those (including myself) who deplored it but thought that it was necessary to face the grim facts. (I suppose it enhances the self-esteem of a scholar, if they can bask in the idea of facing up to facts, however grim.) There were indeed facts that supported the notion of secularization, but, in retrospect, we misinterpreted these facts. Our main mistake was that we misunderstood pluralism as just one factor supporting secularization; in fact, pluralism, the co-existence of different worldviews and value systems in the same society, is *the* major change brought about by modernity for the place of religion both in the minds of individuals and in the institutional order. This may or may not be associated with secularization, but it is independent of it. It does indeed constitute a challenge to religious faith, but it is a *different* challenge from that of secularity. As my teacher Carl Mayer used to say, "Here one must distinguish very sharply!"

It took me some twenty-five years to conclude that secularization theory has turned out to be empirically untenable. I proclaimed my change of mind very noisily in the introduction to a book I edited in 1999, *The Desecularization of the World.* I find it important to emphasize that this change of mind on my part was not due to some philosophical or theological conversion. My religious position, which I have described as incurably Lutheran, has not changed since my youth. What happened to me was much less dramatic: It became more and more apparent that the empirical data contradicted the theory. With some exceptions, notably Europe and an international intelligentsia, our world is anything but secular; it is as religious as ever, and in places more so. (The exceptions have to be explained, and I have made some efforts to do so. For more on this point, see my book with Grace Davie and Effie Fokas, *Religious America, Secular Europe?* 2008.) I was also not alone in my change of mind. Almost everyone studying contemporary religion has replicated it. There is a relatively small group of scholars who continue to defend secularization theory. Of course I disagree with them, but I also have some admiration for them. I have sympathy for people who stubbornly refuse to follow the herd!

In early 2012, rather unexpectedly, a simple idea occurred to me. As happens in such cases, I wondered why the idea had not occurred to me before. It was rather obvious, but its implications kept getting bigger, the more I thought about it. The well-known sociologist Jose Casanova (Georgetown University) has performed a very useful task by taking apart the several meanings of the concept of secularization, some problematic, some not. One meaning that neither Casanova nor anyone else had a problem with was that of *differentiation:* In the course of modernization, for various reasons, societal functions that used to be vested in religious institutions have now become differentiated between the latter and other (mostly new or redefined) institutions – church and state, religion and the economy, religion and education, and so forth. Fair enough, but, as a duly accredited specialist in the sociology of knowledge, I should have recalled a basic insight of this approach: If it is to function in society, every institution must have a correlate in consciousness. Therefore, if a differentiation has occurred between religious and other institutions in society, this differentiation must also be manifested in the consciousness of individuals. In this connection I stumbled across a very interesting phrase coined by the seventeenth-century Dutch jurist Hugo Grotius. He proposed that the new discipline of international law should be developed *"etsi Deus non daretur"* – "as if God were not given" or "as if God did not exist." In other words, he proposed that an entire institution should be divorced from any religious presuppositions and should be dominated by a strictly secular discourse. Once that idea is grasped, a mass of empirical data suddenly makes new sense. Most religious people, even very fervent ones, operate within a secular discourse in important areas of their lives. Put differently, for most believers there is not a stark either/or dichotomy between faith and secularity but rather a fluid construction of both/and. In developing this insight, I have found Alfred Schutz's concepts of "multiple realities" and "relevance structures" very helpful. When thinking along these lines, one gains a much better understanding of important issues in contemporary global religion: the meteoric rise of Evangelicalism (especially in its Pentecostal version) and its positive relation to modernization; the curious overlap between the Bible Belt and the Sun Belt in the United States; and the intense debates across the Muslim world on the relation of Islam and modernity. In looking at the world from this perspective, another helpful concept is Shmuel Eisenstadt's idea of "multiple modernities." Western secularity is not the only form of modernity; there are other versions of modernity, in which religion is accorded a much more central place.

For some time now I have argued that, if secularization theory must be given up, we need a theory of pluralism to replace it. The former theory was a paradigm in its time. The present volume is intended as a modest contribution to a new paradigm. Much more work will be needed to flesh it out. No individual could possibly do this. It will require efforts over some years by colleagues from different disciplines and with different competences.

"A modest contribution"? Proposing a new paradigm may seem anything but modest, an exercise in *chutzpah* if not a symptom of megalomania. I suppose that, like all academics after a certain age, I am not immune to delusions of grandeur. Yet I will say that, in my case, any full surrender to such a delusion has been held in check by an ineradicable sense of the ridiculous. And what is more ridiculous than a professor claiming to be a great sage? Be this as it may, I do believe that I have something useful to say here. As my favorite Zulu proverb puts it: If I don't beat my drum, who will?

The replacement of one theory by another may strike a non-academic as an obscure, impractical exercise. I hope that the following chapters make clear that this is not the case. There are few issues more important internationally than the ongoing "struggle for the soul of Islam," which is raging from North Africa to Southeast Asia. There are two questions in contention. One is intensely personal: "How can I be a pious, practicing Muslim, and at the same time a modern person?" The other is political: "What could and should an Islamic modernity look like?" The two questions must be addressed together. Of course the answers cannot come from social science but must come from religious reflection within the Muslim community. However, since such reflection takes place in social contexts amenable to empirical inquiry, social scientists (even if they are not Muslims) can provide relevant insights. When the AKP, the Islamist party, was elected to power in Turkey, some of its followers said, We don't want an Islamic state. We want to be good Muslims in a secular republic. Whatever happens to this particular experiment, that formulation touches the core of the "theory" aimed for in this book – a project anything but obscure or impractical! Similar questions are being debated in many other parts of the world – China, India, Russia, Israel, secular Europe, and last but not least in the United States.

The British sociologist Steve Bruce is one of the rather small contingent of social scientists who defiantly hold on to secularization theory. In an amicable essay published in 2001 he suggested that I should recant my "unnecessary recantation" of secularization theory and, as it were, return to the fold. I did not accept the suggestion then, and I am not about to accept it now. This is not what I am doing in this book. However, I am now prepared to concede that the secularization theorists are not quite as wrong as I previously thought. I now understand more fully the global reality of the secular discourse, not just in Europe and in faculty clubs all over the world, but in the lives of many ordinary believers who succeed in being *both* secular *and* religious. I would say that it is these people who perform the prototypical cognitive balancing act of modernity and by this act modify the sharp dichotomy between the secularization theorists and those who announce "the return of the gods." In the last chapter of this book I deal with various "formulas of peace" that have sought to ensure the co-existence of different religions in the same society. Perhaps this book could also be seen as proposing a "formula of peace" between contending interpreters of the religious scene.

Chapters one through three elaborate and, to an extent, modify statements I have made before about religion and modernity. Chapters four through six contain the results of my most recent thinking about this topic. Readers will have to decide whether they can go along with me as I develop my argument. I hope that even those who cannot will find the argument interesting and in parts entertaining. I think that it helps to understand religion if one perceives its profoundly comic character – the comedy of this mutant species of the Big Apes trying to discern the ultimate meaning of the galaxies. In any case, I think that the perspective outlined in this book is helpful in grasping the endlessly fascinating reality of the religious landscape and also offers some building blocks for a new paradigm of modernity and religion.

Some acknowledgements are in order. I want to thank Professor Detlef Pollack, who invited me in May 2012 to give the inaugural lecture of the program "Religion and Modernity," which he directs at the University of Muenster, in Germany. This lecture was the first occasion for me to go public with the new ideas that have been occupying me recently. I was greatly encouraged and stimulated by the discussion that followed the lecture. In 2013 Pollack published and edited a brochure with a German translation of my lecture, "After the Demise of Secularization Theory," with a number of commentaries by faculty associated with his program. The original English text, under the title "Further Thoughts on Modernity and Religion," was published in the journal *Society* (July-August 2012). I want to thank its editor, Jonathan Imber, for this and also for his willingness to publish the papers of two conferences on the topic of pluralism held at Boston University's Institute on Culture, Religion and World Affairs (CURA), which I founded in 1985 and with which I am still associated as a senior research fellow. I also want to thank Dan Schmidt of the Lynne and Harry Bradley Foundation, which funded these conferences and has long been a faithful supporter of the work of our Institute. Thanks also to those who invited me to present these ideas – to Professors Thomas Banchoff and Jose Casanova of the Berkley Center at Georgetown University; to Father Gustavo Morello, SJ, of the Jesuit Institute at Boston College; and to Dr. Silke Loechner of the Deutsche Evangelische Kirchentag in Hamburg. Finally, I want to thank Walter Russell Mead, who originally invited me to write a blog on the website of the journal *The American Interest*. I have been writing this blog, "Religion and Other Curiosities," for some three years now. I have come to like this literary genre, a high-tech enhancement of the classical European institution of the newspaper *feuilleton*. It forces one to make one's points very succinctly. Also, the necessity of having something to say about religion every week has forced me to constantly roam around the global religious scene – a great way to get a sense of what is going on and to subject abstract academic theories to the hard tests of ordinary reality.

Chapter 1: The Pluralist Phenomenon

The term "pluralism" has a long history in philosophy, where it has basically meant that there are several ways of looking at reality. In recent philosophical discourse the term has been applied to Ludwig Wittgenstein's concept of "language games." Interesting though this may be, this philosophical usage is not what I am concerned with here. Rather I mean by pluralism a phenomenon, not in the mind of a philosophical thinker, but an empirical fact in society experienced by ordinary people (of whom, happily, there are many more than philosophers). This more mundane meaning of the term was pioneered by Horace Kallen (1882–1974), a Harvard-trained philosopher who taught for many years at the New School for Social Research, which is located in New York's Greenwich Village, a bohemian setting where Kallen could experience a plurality of human types far greater than that of Harvard Yard in his student years. He was the son of a rabbi who came to the United States with his family when Horace was five years old. Long before he encountered philosophy, he lived through the tumultuous reality of the immigrant experience, and he liked it. Thus he not only described but celebrated a multicultural United States. This double meaning of pluralism – as a simple description of social facts and as an ideology – has continued to this day.

I too came to the United States as an immigrant, though I was seventeen rather than five, and I have relished its diversity ever since. But I am writing here as an observer rather than a celebrant. The suffix "ism" of course suggests an ideology, and for a time I used the more descriptive term "plurality" instead. I then found that I had to keep explaining what I was talking about – "you know, like *pluralism.*" The latter term is readily understood and indeed has become part of ordinary language. I am here using the term in its vernacular meaning.

All the same, my use of the term should be clearly defined: Pluralism is a social situation in which people with different ethnicities, worldviews, and moralities live together peacefully and interact with each other amicably. The last phrase is important. It makes little sense to speak of pluralism if people do not talk with each other – for instance, where people do interact but only as masters and slaves, or where they live in sharply segregated communities and only interact in exclusively economic relations. For pluralism to unleash its full dynamic, there must be sustained conversation, not necessarily between equals, but extended in time and covering a broad range of subjects. Anthropologists have two useful terms for this: *commensality* and *connubium*, eating together and/or marrying each other; put differently, we are referring to dinner conversation and/or pillow talk.

What happens then is the process I have called *cognitive contamination*. The phrase may not be a glorious contribution to the English language, but sometimes not sticking to the vernacular has its uses. The phrase refers to a commonly observed fact: If people keep on talking with each other, they will influence each other. Social psychologists have amassed a rich literature about this. Some of it is funny. For example, Milton Rokeach wrote an intriguing book, *The Three Christs of Ypsilanti* (1964). The Ypsilanti in the title is not the Greek city in which the poet Byron died but the location of a mental hospital in Michigan. It had two inmates, each of whom believed himself to be Jesus Christ. They somehow got along, but the psychiatrists became worried when a third patient arrived with the same delusion. To address this concern, the three were not separated but actually put together. Rokeach described what happened: The three invented what can only be described as an ingenious theology, which allowed each of the three to keep his title as some sort of Christ. People who keep talking to each other, even if they are patients in a psychiatric hospital, end up influencing each other; they come to a cognitive compromise.

I am here making two important propositions. The first is that cognitive contamination relativizes; the second is that pluralism produces cognitive contamination as an ongoing condition.

My understanding of cognitive contamination is a footnote to Leon Festinger's very important work on what he called cognitive dissonance (*A Theory of Cognitive Dissonance* 1957). The term refers to what happens when people are presented with alleged facts that contradict what they had previously believed. Festinger was particularly interested in strategies people used to avoid the dissonance. For example, people who smoke will quickly turn to another section of the newspaper when they come upon an article that describes the alleged health hazards of smoking. Interestingly, Festinger wrote about this some years before the outbreak of the great war against tobacco. I don't think that the strategies he described have changed much, except that the dissonance-avoiding smoker now has more articles to skip. According to Festinger, there is a whole scale of avoidance strategies: denying the validity of the dissonant information, which I will call methodological assassination, a favorite tool of social scientists with strong prejudices; attacking the personal motives of the bearers of the information, e. g., they are in the pay of some vested interest or other; physically removing the bearers of the information from the scene or fleeing from the scene oneself; or in extreme cases converting them or killing them. There is also another option: negotiate with them. That of course is what the inmates of Rokeach's mental hospital did. I have called this cognitive bargaining. It is a very important strategy as one tries to understand pluralism.

Any extended interaction with others who disagree with one's own view of the world relativizes the latter. Those who hold conflicting views don't even have to say anything about the disagreement – just sitting together can be upsetting. Let me stay with the smoking example. Many children today are thoroughly indoctrinated in the belief that smoking is very harmful. This belief is supported in families as well as by school programs, health professionals, and the media. I once experienced a relativizing incident in this area. A little girl who had clearly been indoctrinated into anti-smoking virtue was in her parents' living room when a visitor sat down and lit his pipe. No one objected; this was in the early days of this particular culture war. The little girl froze in her seat, her eyes open wide. It was clear that she was deeply shocked. In the event the offending visitor said nothing. But suppose that the girl had recovered from her freeze and challenged the smoker: "Don't you know that smoking is bad for your health?" Suppose that he had replied, "No. I don't think so," and calmly gone on enjoying his pipe. One can imagine any number of further scenarios, up to physical violence. The basic point here is quite simple: Relativization occurs, at least minimally, when someone visibly behaves differently from what someone else had taken for granted as proper behavior. The relativization intensifies if the challenger verbalizes the disagreement. Thus various forms of interaction with different worldviews and the behaviors they engender initiate a process of relativization.

Another example of this process is found in the work of Montesquieu, who was a rather unreliable but nonetheless enormously influential political thinker. In his book *The Persian Letters* (1721), Montesquieu provides a good illustration of the point I want to make here. The book contains letters supposedly sent back home by two Persian visitors to Paris. They express astonishment at what they are discovering in the circles among which they move, for example about the co-existence of monogamy and adultery, which they find odd. They also report on the astonishment voiced by the locals regarding what the visitors tell them about life back in Persia, for example, about polygamy and harems. The Parisians ask, "How can one be a Persian?" But the question that Montesquieu really wants to raise is, "How can one be a Parisian?" That, precisely, is relativization, which is what Montesquieu intended; it is the insight that reality can be perceived and lived differently from what one had thought of as the only way. Or, put simply, things can be really, really different. Anthropologists call this experience "culture shock," and a good number of anthropologists deal with the relativizing shock by "going native." Pluralism brings about a situation in which relativization becomes a permanent experience. This can occur on very different levels of sophistication – that of a little girl witnessing what for her constitutes outrageous behavior, or that of an anthropologist trying to construct a theory of cannibalism.

Pluralism, as I have defined it, has existed in different forms at various points in history. It has been a long tradition in the cultures of East Asia, notably China and Japan. Pre-Islamic India exemplified pluralism in a somewhat different way. For several centuries the countries along the Silk Road demonstrated an exuberant religious pluralism, with Christians, Manicheans, Zoroastrians, Hindus, Buddhists, and Confucian scholars interacting with each other, often in the context of the Hellenistic states left behind as a legacy of the eastern conquests of Alexander the Great. A wonderful example of this sort of conversation is a classic Buddhist text, *The Questions of King Milinda*, which contains a dialogue between a Buddhist sage and a Hellenistic ruler, whose Greek name was probably Menander. This Hellenistic king asks questions about Buddhism from the perspective of his own experience with Greek philosophy. It is a wonderful example of two very different worldviews, both of which are very religious in different ways, having to come to terms with each other. Hellenism, which flourished in the urban centers of the late Roman Empire, was a very distinctive form of pluralism and was very important for the course of European civilization. It was in that favorable context that Christianity spread out from its original location, beginning with the Apostle Paul's mission to Athens, where Paul directly addressed this Hellenistic pluralism in his sermon reported in the Book of Acts: "Men of Athens, I perceive that in every way you are very religious. For as I passed along, and observed the objects of your worship, I found also an altar with this inscription, 'To an unknown god.' What therefore you worship as unknown, this I proclaim to you." He then proclaimed the Gospel of Jesus Christ, whose worship was central to Paul's faith. There were periods (some short, others longer) in the history of Islam when rulers permitted and even encouraged religious and cultural pluralism, as in Muslim Spain, Moghul India, and the Ottoman Empire; in the first case a special term, *conviviencia*, was coined to denote amicable co-existence between Muslims, Christians, and Jews. The Christian Middle Ages in Europe, a historical period not famous for tolerance, also had pluralistic episodes. One example of this is the rule of the Hohenstaufen in Sicily; another is the Langue d'Oc in what is now southern France, which was ruled by the Count of Toulouse, who was himself Catholic but tolerated and even protected the Albigensians until a particularly ferocious crusade from the north exterminated the Albigensian heresy and in the process destroyed the pluralistic culture.

Pluralism is often associated with cities – seats of government, commercial centers, and seaports. An old German adage refers to this fact: *Stadtluft macht frei* , or "city air makes free." There is no great mystery about this. Cities are most often the places where people from very different backgrounds rub shoulders with each other and cognitive contamination begins its creative or (depending on your point of view) destructive job. It is useful to reflect that there were great cities in pre-modern history, just think of Alexandria, and that pluralism is much older than the printing press and the steam engine, two powerful agents of modern pluralism. Modernity can most succinctly be defined as the changes brought about by the science and the technology created in the last few centuries – an ever-accelerating process, with consequences affecting ever more areas of human life. In a way, modernization means a sort of expanding urbanization, so that more and more people throughout the world come to breathe "city air," even if many of them still live in places that are not, or not yet, cities. Pluralism thus becomes globalized. In a way, the whole planet becomes an enormous city.

Modernization leads to a huge transformation in the human condition from fate to choice. We may assume that the capacity to make choices is intrinsic to *homo sapiens* and that, as far back as the first appearance of our species, individuals could make some choices. ("Shall I hunt lions on this side of the river or on the other side?") But the range of choices increases through history and has increased exponentially since the Industrial Revolution. This transformation has been basically the product of a vast enhancement of technology, such as the steam engine and what follows it, which itself was made possible by the development of what we now know as modern science, a cognitive revolution disseminated by way of the printing press. We can visualize Neolithic people sitting in their caves and banging away with a crude hammer on the lion carcass they dragged in. The banging went on for centuries, with the same kind of hammer. Now we have not only a wide range of tools to choose from but entire alternative systems of technology. Far beyond technology, we can now choose whom to marry and how many children to have, our occupation and place of residence, our form of political and economic organization, our means of entertainment, our objects of worship (especially of course in contexts where there is a measure of religious freedom), and even our identity (as in the modern mantra, "I want to find out who I am"). This is an interesting way of putting things, because it uses the language of fate ("who I am") to convey an understanding of a person's choosing who they are. All of life becomes an interminable process of redefining who the individual is in the context of the seemingly endless possibilities presented by modernity. This endless array of choices is reinforced by the structures of capitalist systems, with their enormous market for services, products, and even identities, all protected by a democratic state which legitimates these choices, not least the choice of religion. All of these areas of an individual's life were once taken for granted, were fated. They now become an arena of almost endless choices.

The writings of the German social theorist Arnold Gehlen (1904–1976) are useful in understanding this process of expanding choices. Human beings, compared with other mammals, have a relatively meager repertoire of instincts telling them what to do. Long before the advent of modernity, this biological fact forced the human individual to reflect and to choose. If a choice had to be made every time a course of action is to be undertaken, the individual would be overwhelmed by indecision. (In that case, we may imagine, a lion would eat *him* rather than the other way around, which would lead to a very poor prognosis for the future of the species in the savage competition of the evolutionary process.) To make up for the meagerness of human instincts, *institutions* were developed. Institutions provide the programs of action that instincts fail to provide. That is, they erect an area of stability where the individual can act almost automatically and without much reflection, and at the same time they make possible another area in which the individual is free to make choices. Gehlen called these two areas, respectively, the background and the foreground of human social life. The background is strongly institutionalized, the foreground is de-institutionalized; the background is the realm of fate, the foreground that of choices. Konrad Lorenz, the zoologist who created the discipline of "ethology," was particularly interested in what he called "triggers" – the stimuli that provoke this or that instinct to spring into consciousness and lead to the appropriate behavior. Female mammals have an instinct to feed their newborn offspring. Lorenz wanted to discover the trigger that provoked feeding behavior in one particular species of birds, the so-called grey geese, which he studied for many years. He wanted to stimulate the trigger himself so that the mother goose would feed *him*. He eliminated visual triggers, consisting of various physical signals. He finally concluded that the trigger is audial – a particular chirping sound. When the mother goose hears this sound, she swoops down and feeds the infant. Lorenz finally succeeded in being fed himself. He made a film of this experience, in which Lorenz, a very large, hairy man, is busily chirping away. Mother goose could not possibly have looked at him and mistaken him for her baby goose, but she heard the chirping sound and promptly came down and fed the big human who had produced the correct trigger. One way of explaining Gehlen's concept of institutions is to refer to them as artificial triggers.

If Gehlen's anthropological assumptions are correct, and I think they are, then this has always been so. It had to be, or social life could not go on. If society were all "background," we would be programmed like robots – a biological impossibility, as anyone who has ever dealt with young children will readily understand; they have a way of resisting the behavior that their elders want to instill in them, at least for a while. If, on the other hand, society were all "foreground," we would have to make new choices every day and social life would come to a grinding halt. If this is a bit too abstract, let me give an illustration I have often used in teaching. We are assembled for a seminar in which, say, we are to discuss the theories of Arnold Gehlen. I have taught seminars many times, and most of the students have been in seminars before. We know the rules; we don't have to re-negotiate them every time we meet. We take these rules so much for granted that we must pause to recollect what they are. Let me spell out some of them: We will all sit around this table, we will not hold hands and dance around it. However much we may disagree, there will be no physical violence. There will be no overt sexual activity. There will be no spitting, urinating, or defecating in this room. Now just imagine that these rules, which are part of the *institution* of higher education in the United States, were not there as a background for our gathering. We would have to re-negotiate all these rules every time we meet; let's vote – sitting down or dancing? Sexual activity, yes or no? Apart from the fact that this would be emotionally intolerable, we would never get to the actual agenda of the seminar: After all the rules had been re-negotiated, no time would be left for Gehlen! Those of us old enough to have lived through the so-called student revolution of the late 1960s can recall the tedium of the open-ended talk sessions that were supposedly required for democratic decision-making. We also know that the stable institutional background of an academic seminar can be verbally and behaviorally challenged; perhaps not every one of the above rules, but many of those that were previously taken for granted as defining the roles of professors and students. Gehlen called such challenges *de-institutionalization*. They occurred frequently in the late sixties in American and European universities. Of course this allegedly democratic chaos did not last; it couldn't. After a while, new institutional programs were devised. The university changed as a result, but it survived in its basic functions, e.g., to transmit bodies of knowledge and to serve as a holding pen for notoriously misbehaving young humans. Max Weber had a phrase for this process: the "routinization of charisma." "Routinization" is a good translation of his German *Veralltaeglichung*, which literally means "everyday-ization". Charisma is the force that challenges and disrupts everyday routines. It cannot last; new institutional patterns eventually emerge.

An episode from that period may be useful in illustrating this process. As I recall, it was at a conference in Washington in the early 1970s. A session was rudely and loudly disrupted by some radicals in the audience. I noticed that someone from the organizing committee sat a row or so from the main disrupter. When the disruption occurred, he got up and suggested a special session to discuss the topic demanded by the radicals. I concluded that the conference *apparatchik* had expected the disruption and had his response ready. In other words, what I was witnessing was a pre-arranged, possibly scheduled disruption. I could imagine an exchange of notes between the two interlocutors: "If it's okay, we'll disrupt the session at 10:15am." "Fine. I'll be ready to respond. How about scheduling the session you want for tomorrow at 11:30?" Higher education in the United States and Europe survived these turbulent years by precisely this sort of collusion between revolutionaries and bureaucrats. The end result is typically that the revolutionaries become bureaucrats themselves.

Pluralism is not the only factor in the multiplication of choices, but it is a very important one. Using Gehlen's terms, pluralism greatly helps the expansion of the "foreground" at the expense of the "background." This is very obvious in the area of religion, which is the major concern of this book. Let us look at another area, that of gender relations. Here it has been the feminism of recent provenance that has reduced the area of taken-for-grantedness and enabled, indeed compelled individuals to make choices. Leaving aside more titillating instances of sexual behavior, let us take an example of ordinary social etiquette: a well-behaved, middle-class American male approaching a door in the company of a woman. Not so long ago he would, without the need for reflection, have held the door open and let her go through ahead of him. He would not have to worry about her reaction. He might actually say, "Ladies first." In other words, this mundane bit of social interaction had long ago been institutionalized. Now the situation is different. If the man doesn't know the woman well, he must quickly reflect as to what type of reaction he is likely to receive, as de-institutionalized reactions may range from grateful to hostile. Let's assume that he doesn't know much about the woman in question. As he must quickly decide what to do, the man has to try to place the woman in a cultural typology he carries around in his head. If all he knows is that she is the elderly president of the local Republican club, he may decide to bet on old-fashioned courtesy. If he knows that she is a middle-aged professor of sociology, he will more likely follow the etiquette of gender equality. In any case, he is faced with a typical consequence of de-institutionalization.

Gehlen understood something else about institutions, which is that their deconstruction at first brings about an exhilarating sense of liberation. European and American literature is full of stories about individuals who come to a big city from narrow provincial places, where suddenly new horizons open up and old repressions are overcome. One can exuberantly dance around the tree of liberty. After a while, however, the dizziness of liberation gives way to mounting anxiety. It is as if there is no ground to stand on; nothing is certain, and there are no more reliable guides to how one ought to live. One now seeks a new liberation, a liberation *from* the previous liberation that had done away with the old institutional constraints. Typically what follows is the reconstruction of institutions, whether old or new. The psychology underlying this development is nicely expressed in an old American joke: Two friends meet after not having seen each other for a while. "How are you? Are you still unemployed?" "No, I have a job now. But it is a terrible job." "What is the job?" "Well, I work in an orange grove. I sit in the shade, under a tree. Oranges are brought to me, and I must sort them into three baskets – one for big oranges, one for little oranges, and one for in-between oranges. That is what I do all day long." "I don't understand. This sounds to me like a pleasant job. Why do you say it is terrible?" "*All those decisions!*"

Pluralism relativizes and thereby undermines many of the certainties by which human beings used to live. Put differently, certainty becomes a scarce commodity. I do not want to get into the question whether there is a deep need for certainty implanted in human nature. Empirically, such a need appears to be widely diffused, and those who have it get very upset if the need is frustrated. It seems to me that this why so many modern people are anxious, and incidentally why the calm certainty of pre-modern societies is attractive and becomes a utopia for a lot of nervous moderns, including anthropologists who "go native." The dream of Shangri-la persists. There are two seemingly opposite but actually profoundly similar attempts to allay the anxiety brought on by relativization: fundamentalism and relativism. I have dealt with this topic in detail in a book I wrote with Anton Zijderveld, *In Praise of Doubt* (2009). I am not assuming that readers of this book are familiar with earlier scribblings of mine, so I will briefly go over this ground again. As the legendary Rabbi Meir of Vilna put it so well: "If I don't plagiarize from myself, from whom should I plagiarize"?

Fundamentalism is an effort to restore the threatened certainty. The term is usually applied to religious movements, but it is important to understand that there are many secular fundamentalisms – political, philosophical, aesthetic, even culinary (as in the case of some vegetarians) or athletic (as in allegiance to a particular sports team). Just about any idea or practice can become the foundation of a fundamentalist project, on very different levels of sophistication – as, for example, in the similarities and differences between a Marxist theorist and a fanatical believer in weight reduction. Also, the project may be to go back to a (real or imagined) certainty in the past (for example, traditional Catholicism) or to look in an attitude of assurance toward the future (as in the case of most modern revolutionary movements). In other words, there are reactionary and progressive fundamentalisms. What all these projects have in common is a promise to the potential convert: "Come join us, and you will have the certainty you have long desired. You will understand the world, you will know who you are, and you will know how to live." Of course an observer may think that this or that project is based on illusion, but this is neither here nor there. If the invitation to join is accepted, the promise of redemptive certainty is likely to be fulfilled. *If* you are willing to accept the cognitive and normative assumptions of the project, and *if* you can continue to do so over time, you will indeed live with a new sense of conviction. But this sense will be vulnerable, as compared to the tranquil conviction of pre-modern humanity.

A closer look at reactionary fundamentalism will make this clearer. There is a great difference between tradition and neo-traditionalism. For pre-modern human beings, worldview and value-system are taken for granted, and no reflection or decision is necessary. Of course there may be strictures directed against outsiders, but people firmly rooted in a tradition can afford a certain amount of tolerance toward those who don't share the tradition. Neo-traditionalists cannot afford such tolerance. For them the tradition is not simply given, they have *chosen* it – and they cannot forget this. Consequently they may loudly affirm the tradition, just as the genuine pre-modern person once did, but there will be an undertone of uncertainty that makes for a very different situation. Fundamentalists are aggressive in the same measure as they are vulnerable.

An example of this is a comparison of Orthodox Jews in a traditional *shtetl* in eastern Europe, say in the old Pale of Settlement in Russia, with Orthodox Jews in the United States today. In the first instance, the Orthodox identity and all that went with it in terms of worldview and behavior was simply given. Undoubtedly there were some eccentric individuals who were dissidents within the community, but they were unlikely to threaten its stability. The Gentile world outside could certainly be threatening physically, but if anything that would only strengthen the cohesion of the community. As the Yiddish adage had it, it was "hard to be a Jew," but there was no plausible escape from that destiny. There are also Orthodox Jews in the contemporary United States. The more radical groups have constructed communities that seem like replicas of the old *shtetl*, for instance in some neighborhoods of Brooklyn. An individual born and raised there may find it psychologically difficult to escape, but there are no physical or legal barriers imposed from outside. Another previously secular individual who joined the community as a convert will find it easier to leave again. However, neither individual can eradicate from their consciousness the fact that they are there by choice, be it the choice to stay or the choice to join. The choices can be reversed, and they know it. All they have to do is get on the subway and leave for Manhattan. This example could also be transferred to Israel. Certain neighborhoods in Jerusalem, like Meah Shearim, also seem like transplanted Russian *shtetls*, but they are not. One can walk out, get on a bus, and move to Tel Aviv.

To further underline the difference between tradition and neo-traditionalism, let me mention a story that has nothing to do with religion. The Empress

Eugenie of France, wife of Napoleon III, came from rather lowly origins and had a shady past before she was elevated to her imperial status. On a state visit to London Eugenie was taken to the opera by Queen Victoria, whose royal origins were of course impeccable. Both women cut impressive figures. Eugenie, the guest, entered the royal box first, regally acknowledged the applause of the public, graciously looked behind herself, and sat down. She was followed by Victoria, who also regally responded to the applause and sat down. She did not look behind herself. She knew that the chair would be there.

Relativism can be simply defined as the embrace of relativity; that is, the relativization that has in fact occurred is celebrated as a superior form of knowledge. One cannot be certain about anything because there *is* no absolute cognitive or normative truth. In other words, the experience of relativity, which terrifies fundamentalists and from which they seek to escape, now becomes an insight to be proud of and to apply to the practice of living. Like fundamentalism, relativism can be found on different levels of sophistication. It can be formulated in theories developing what Nietzsche called "the art of mistrust." The basic method here is to translate affirmations of truth or virtue into expressions of allegedly underlying interests that have nothing to do with truth or virtue – interests of power, or greed, or lust. Machiavelli, Marx, and Freud are major representatives of this type of worldview. They have not only served to legitimate extant relativity, but they have engendered political and cultural movements from which followers could derive programs of behavior. So-called postmodernism has been a recent theoretical flowering of this worldview. However, the same basic worldview can be held in much less philosophically sophisticated ways, by individuals who may not have considered the theoretical underpinnings of cultural realities. These individuals regularly voice opinions that may be called mantras of relativism. The American language, reflecting a society that has long been in the vanguard of pluralism, has produced a lexicon of popular wisdom that is at hand when an occasion calls for it: "Says you!" "We'll agree to disagree." "It's a free country." This practical relativism may not be supported by a body of theory but simply by the pretention that the individual who spouts this wisdom refuses to share the illusions of others or to be taken in by their rhetoric. Such individuals may simply relish their cynicism. If they espouse any virtue at all, it will be an all-embracing tolerance. I suppose if one wanted to set up categories of classification here, one might distinguish between kindly and nasty relativists: "I respect you despite our differences," as opposed to, "You think this way because you are an asshole, and I am not." The two categories share the same epistemology.

Relativists with theoretical aspirations have one basic problem: How to explain why they alone see reality as it really is, while everyone else is stumbling around in a fog of illusions. What is needed now is a theory of false consciousness (why you are an asshole) and of cognitive privilege (why I am not). Some of these attempts can be quite funny. For example, the history of Marxism can be seen as the extended comedy of a Quixotic quest for a cognitively privileged elite. Marx thought that the proletariat had such a privileged view of reality because its condition of exploitation as it were burned away the false consciousness of the bourgeoisie and thus made it possible for the proletariat to become a revolutionary class. It was left unexplained how Marx, a bourgeois if there ever was one, married to an aristocrat and financially dependent on a capitalist friend, managed to escape the false consciousness of his class. Unfortunately the proletariat in the developed capitalist societies failed to develop the revolutionary consciousness proposed by Marxist theory. Lenin thought up an ingenious theory to deal with this problem: The proletariat may be stuck in the false consciousness that made it eschew revolution for social-democratic reforms within the capitalist system, but the revolutionary party was the "vanguard of the proletariat;" therefore the "party is always right," a maxim that legitimated the Communists' role in creating the Soviet dictatorship. This notion of the party as vanguard was duly adopted by Communist parties outside Russia. Unfortunately, not only was the behavior of "real existing socialism" (as against the humane claims of its ideology) morally repulsive, but these regimes were obviously trapped in illusions all their own. Other cognitive elites had to be discovered. Two that have resonated into our own time were invented by two Marxist thinkers in the first half of the twentieth century. The fiery German revolutionary Rosa Luxemburg, later murdered by right-wing death squads, argued that what she called "the colonial peoples" constituted an "external proletariat" with (she hoped) the requisite revolutionary consciousness. This particular theoretical construction eventually led to the notion of the "Third World," which continues to inspire Marxists and quasi-Marxists today. In Latin America this ideology has been called *tercermundismo* by its critics. The Italian Communist Antonio Gramsci, imprisoned by Mussolini under conditions that allowed him to write, argued that the true revolutionary class would be the intelligentsia. That theory, whether they knew it or not, inspired the student rebels of the late sixties, who broke all the rules of the academic institution by, among other transgressions, defecating in the dean's office. I could go on, but perhaps the point has been made.

It would obviously be a big mistake to think that most people in a modern society are either fundamentalists or relativists. Most people are not in the business of reflection, let alone theorizing. They reflect when they have to – that is, when a problem arises that directly affects their ordinary lives – and they leave theorizing to those whose professions assign this task to them. In other words, most people live in the middle ground between denying and celebrating relativity. They manage to live in the pluralistic situation by managing it pragmatically. They engage in a *conviviencia* with the "others" in their social environment, avoiding direct contradictions and striking bargains on the basis of live-and-let-live. These bargains may or may not involve cognitive compromises between worldviews and values. It is actually surprising how effective and long-lasting such a way of life can be. However, it is also surprising how quickly it can be disrupted, usually by political leaders who use ethnic or religious hatred for their own purposes. The wars following the breakup of the Yugoslav state provide a depressing lesson in this.

Compared to other societies, the United States has been relatively successful in managing pluralism. Of course this has been greatly facilitated by the ideology of the American creed and its legal establishment. However, the managing of pluralism is practiced daily by people who don't recite the Bill of Rights at breakfast. Take a stable working-class family in a contemporary American city. Make them, say, Italian-American. The husband runs a reasonably successful electrician business, and the family is financially comfortable. When asked their religion, they will say "Catholic." The wife does indeed go to mass fairly regularly, but she could not be described as pious. The husband is an amiable agnostic; he has no relationship with the local parish. The couple never discusses religion. Other than in the area of culinary preferences, their Italian ethnicity means little to them. They have two children. The boy is still in high school; he is a fair student, but his time is mostly occupied with video games, athletics, and pornographic fantasies. The daughter, brighter than her little brother, is a sophomore at the local state university. She has been fascinated by one of her teachers, who exudes a semi-sophisticated mix of feminist and postmodern jargon. The young woman brings some of this back home, equally upsetting both of her parents, who don't quite know how to deal with this. The situation gets more complicated. The most sought-after young man in the daughter's class is the handsome son of immigrants from Pakistan. His parents are moderately observant Muslims, far from any kind of fundamentalism, and their son was raised without much contact with the local mosque. However, he and some friends of his have been fascinated of late by a popular online imam, who is also not a fundamentalist but is an advocate of a decidedly Islamic identity and lifestyle. The young man has been attending Friday prayers (his parents are uneasy about this) and is thinking of growing a beard. This road toward Mecca has been abruptly interrupted by the two young people being thrown together at a school event. The attraction has been fierce and mutual. They now see each other every day. The hormones are raging. Nothing too serious has, as yet, been happening on the erotic front, but things seem to be heading that way. Both sets of parents are aware of the situation and are quite upset by it. One can imagine different further scenarios, some involving compromises between feminist, Islamic, and (perhaps) Catholic discourses, and some simply pragmatic – a tearful separation, a surreptitious affair, an interfaith wedding. Whatever happens, all stakeholders in this drama will have to face up to the challenge of pluralism in a way they did not have to before.

The grandparents of the couple, back in a village in Sicily or in provincial Pakistan, never had to encounter such a challenge. Courtship and generally relations between the sexes were firmly institutionalized. By contrast, the pluralist situation into which immigration plunged these people is *de*-institutionalized. Of course it is liberating – new horizons are opening up all around. The situation is also *individuating*. The individual is thrown back upon himself or herself, to choose and decide and keep to the course decided upon. That is quite an assignment. The traditional sources of social support are greatly weakened or altogether absent – family, extended kinship, village community, clan, tribe or caste, church or mosque. Somehow individuals must construct their own little programs for the business of living. Earlier I drew attention to the role of cities, long before the modern era, in fostering pluralism. Cities have also always been individuating, making a place for eccentric and sophisticated characters. Such individuals have been called *urbane*. The pluralist situation is thus marked by *urbanity*. The urbane character of modern people is the opposite of what Marx called "the idiocy of village life." Our young lovers, in stark contrast to their grandparents, are all these things – deracinated, individualized, sophisticated – and very nervous!

De-institutionalization forces individuals to undertake the difficult and anxiety-provoking task of building their own little world. They need help. Modern society has developed an array of agencies to provide such help. Gehlen called them *secondary institutions*; they fill the gap left over from de-institutionalization. They offer the individual different programs to cope with various contingencies. Since they lack the taken-for-granted quality of the old primary institutions, they are more fragile and less reliable. Nevertheless they alleviate the burden of individual world-construction. I suppose the principle here would be that any program is better than none. American society, ever the vanguard of pluralism, has been especially prolific in generating such help-giving agencies. There exists a vast network of help organizations and professions – psychiatrists, psychotherapists, social workers, unaccredited "life coaches," gurus, and support groups. Some are supplied by the welfare state, others by non-profit organizations. Some can be purchased on the market. There is also a huge supply of books and Internet websites offering advice of every conceivable sort. I would think that the two young people in my story would be sophisticated enough to find a place that specializes in giving advice in just the situation in which they find themselves, perhaps a "diversity counselor" at their school.

Modernization unleashes all the forces that make for pluralism — urbanization, mass migration (including mass tourism), general literacy and higher education for increasing numbers, and all the recent technologies of communication. In our globalized modernity, almost everyone talks with everyone else, whether directly or indirectly. With the exception of some as-yet isolated tribes in deepest Amazonia, most of our contemporaries are aware of the fact that there are different ways of life, different values, different worldviews. Sooner or later, they will be plunged into the vortex of the pluralist dynamic. To that extent, they will become more like people who live in modernized, pluralistic societies. I think that one should not prematurely deplore or celebrate this development. Like most changes in history, it is a mixed bag.

So far I have said little about religion, which is my main concern in this book. I have tried to give a picture of pluralism and its consequences. The first thing to say about religion is that it is in no way immune to these consequences. I would go further and argue that pluralism is the one overriding challenge to every religious tradition and community in the modern age. In his book *The Joyful Wisdom* (1882), Nietzsche proclaimed the death of God. On the cusp of the twentieth century, he evoked a vision of empty, deserted altars. This is not what in fact occurred. Instead, the last century saw an enormous proliferation of altars. The proliferation continues.

Does it matter? It matters very much. Pluralism in the most comprehensive sense – the co-existence of different ethnic, moral, and religious communities in one society – poses a vitally important political problem. Both fundamentalism and relativism make the problem intractable. Fundamentalism balkanizes a society, leading either to ongoing conflict or to totalitarian coercion. Relativism undermines the moral consensus without which no society can survive. The political problem of pluralism can only be solved by the maintenance and legitimation of the middle ground between these two extremes. For most of humanity, religion determines how one looks at the world and how one should live. That is why the relation of religion and pluralism should be of interest for everyone, regardless of one's own religious beliefs or the absence thereof. The rest of this book will address this topic.

Further Reading

Banchoff, Thomas, ed. *Religious Pluralism, Globalization, and World Politics.* New York: Oxford University Press, 2008.

Berger, Peter L., and Anton Zijderveld. *In Praise of Doubt: How to Have Convictions without Becoming a Fanatic*. New York: HarperOne, 2009.

Festinger, Leon. *A Theory of Cognitive Dissonance*. Stanford: Stanford University Press, 1957.

Gehlen, Arnold. *Man: His Nature and Place in the World*. Translated by Clare McMillan and Karl Pillemer. New York: Columbia University Press, 1988.

Kallen, Horace M. *Cultural Pluralism and the American Idea: An Essay in Social Philosophy*. Philadelphia: University of Pennsylvania Press, 1956.

Kaufmann, Walter. *Nietzsche: Philosopher, Psychologist, Antichrist*. Princeton: Princeton University Press, 1974.

Lorenz, Konrad. *The Foundations of Ethology: The Principal Ideas and Discoveries in Animal Behavior*. Translated by R.W. Kickert. New York: Simon and Schuster, 1982.

Montesquieu. *Persian Letters*. Translated by Margaret Mauldon. New York: Oxford University Press, 2008.

Robbins, Thomas, and Dick Anthony. *In Gods We Trust: New Patterns of Religious Pluralism in America*. New Brunswick: Transaction Publishers, 1990.

Rokeach, Milton. *The Three Christs of Ypsilanti*. New York: New York Review Books, 2011.

Chapter 2: Pluralism and Individual Faith

There have been erudite debates over the concept of religion. Given the great variety of phenomena subsumed under this concept, does it make sense to use the concept at all? I must confess that I find this question sublimely uninteresting. Every concept can be taken apart to show that it does not reflect the complex reality it is intended to delineate. For example, one can define the species *homo sapiens* in terms of the specific traits that distinguish it from the other large apes – among them, erect gait and the absence of a tail. But then, who knows, we may come upon a previously undiscovered tribe whose members have all the traits of humans, but who move around on all fours and display a magnificent tail. The discovery then opens up interesting hypotheses and research agendas regarding what has caused the atypical characteristics of this tribe. No concept can possibly cover all cases. Every concept is an arbitrary construct (Max Weber called it an "ideal type"), which never corresponds fully with reality but which is useful insofar as it allows us to classify real phenomena and to find out empirically where the classifications break down. Thus both Buddhism and Christianity can be usefully defined as being instances of "religion;" having so defined them, we can then proceed to show how, nevertheless, they differ in very important ways. The general concept is still useful in indicating how both variants differ from, say, musical or culinary preferences. I think we can continue to use something close to the commonsensical understanding of religion – a belief that there is a reality beyond the reality of ordinary experience, and that this reality is of great significance for human life. If so, we can further distinguish between two crucial aspects of religion: religion in the consciousness and behavior of individuals and religion in collective institutions. I will look at the former in this chapter and at the latter in the next.

How does modernity affect religion? At least since the eighteenth century, it was generally assumed that it does. The thinkers of the Enlightenment, especially in its French version, were delighted. Religion was equated with superstition; it would be swept away in the bright light of reason. The new age was ceremonially inaugurated during the French Revolution when a *fille de joie* was crowned as the goddess of reason in what had been the Catholic Church of the Madeleine in Paris. Other thinkers, Catholic ones in the forefront, shared the assumption of the anti-religious effect of modernity. They fought it as best as they could. Yet others, who so to speak had no dog in this fight, neither celebrated nor deplored the alleged secularity of the modern age; they just wanted to analyze it objectively. Among them was Max Weber (1864–1920), one of the founders of modern sociology, who also believed that modernity had a negative effect on religion. He called this "the disenchantment of the world," as modern rationality swept away the old mysteries.

The French philosopher Auguste Comte (1798–1857) was very much a (somewhat delayed) child of the Enlightenment, though he tried to mitigate its politically disruptive consequences. He divided history into three phases: the theological, the metaphysical, and the "positive." The last of these, which gave the name of "positivism" to his philosophy, was to be the age of scientific reason. Comte invented the science he called "sociology," which was to be the reigning discipline for this era, including the supplier of its moral foundation. I suppose that Comte can also serve as an exhibit for the proposition that less-than-profound thinkers can have enormous influence. For reasons I am not aware of, his positivism became very important in Brazil, whose flag is still emblazoned by Comte's motto "Order and Progress" in Portuguese translation. He influenced a number of the founders of sociology in Britain and the United States, and his Enlightened prejudices reverberate in the classical school of sociology in France, whose leading figure was Emile Durkheim (1858–1917). Durkheim was far more empirically oriented than Comte (more "positive," if you will), but he also thought that sociology could give the moral guidance for society that religion used to provide. In the wake of the victory of the Left in the culture war that erupted over the Dreyfus affair, a sharp separation of church and state was established in France in 1905. The question arose of how to replace the moral instruction in schools that the Catholic catechism used to offer – in other words, how to design a republican catechism. Durkheim served on the commission that produced a textbook entitled "Manual of Sociology and Morality."

Thus we can see that from the beginnings of modern social science there continued to be an Enlightenment bias concerning religion. This was not necessarily anti-religious in a philosophical way but rather in the assumption that modernity and religion were antagonistic in empirical fact – put simply, the more modernity, the less religion. If one throws Marx in with Durkheim and Weber as the third founding father of sociology, the bias can be seen as even more pervasive. Thus so-called "secularization theory," as it came to be called by social scientists around the 1950s, stood in a long tradition of modern thought about religion. Recently more and more social scientists have given up this theory. I was among them. It might be useful to give a brief account of my own trajectory in this matter – not because it was in any way unusual, but precisely because it was not.

When I started my career as a sociologist of religion, I simply assumed the validity of what was then (in the 1960s) a scholarly consensus – secularization, in the sense of a decline of religion, was an inevitable consequence of modernity. It should be emphasized that this consensus was shared both by individuals who deplored it (most of them themselves religious) and others who identified the alleged secularization with progressive rationality. (A full disclosure is probably appropriate at this point: My own religious position has not significantly changed since my youth; it is a position best described as a nervous Christianity, in the form of a theologically very liberal Lutheranism. The development of my sociological understanding of religion had nothing to do with any theological or philosophical changes in my own worldview.) Most religious commentators on the alleged secularization, myself included, saw it as a serious challenge to faith, one that had to be honestly confronted. There was indeed a rather short-lived movement whose proponents, the so-called "death of God" theologians, actually welcomed the demise of any notion of supernatural reality as a culmination of Christian faith. If ever there was a theological version of a man-bites-dog story, this was it. It did not last very long.

It took me quite a few years to reach the conclusion that secularization theory was empirically untenable. Three experiences influenced this change of mind. Beginning in the late 1960s, my interests as a sociologist came to focus on what used to be called the "Third World," first on Latin America, then on Asia and Africa. It is impossible to spend any time in those societies without being impressed by their pervasive religiosity. The same period saw the rise of the so-called "counterculture" in the United States and Europe. As a friend of mine once put it, it takes a "godder" to smell out a "godder:" I had developed a pretty good nose for religious phenomena, and the place of religion in the "Age of Aquarius" hit me from early on. Then, independently of the other experiences, I had my first contact with the Evangelical community in the United States. Here is a large and intensely religious population in one of the most modern countries in the world – a fact which is hard to interpret as the exception that proves the rule. Slowly and gradually, my writings as a sociologist came to reflect my developing view of religion in the contemporary world. It culminated very noisily in a book I edited in 1999, *The Desecularization of the World*.

One way of describing secularization theory is to say that it was a very Eurocentric view of the world. It is not only that Europe is the most influential part of the world that is indeed strongly secularized, but even in the United States and among Western-educated individuals everywhere the respectable intellectual discourse has been shaped by the European history of ideas. When social scientists travel, they mostly associate with people like themselves, just as other tourists do; taxi drivers and hotel clerks don't count. This is actually true at home; Harvard professors do not have a habit of attending the Pentecostal churches of Brazilian immigrants. Science is often cited as the principal cause of secularization. The scientific understanding of reality supposedly marginalizes religion and eventually makes it incredible. I was never terribly impressed by this interpretation. Most modern people are crucially affected by the technological revolution that modern science has brought about, but scientific reasoning does not dominate the way they think in ordinary life. I did think that some of the basic processes of modernity – industrialization, urbanization, migration, education – pushed religion out of much of the institutional order. I also thought that pluralism, along the lines defined in the previous chapter, also fostered secularization – it deprived religion of its taken-for-granted quality. That was a correct insight. However, I made an important mistake: Pluralism undermines religious certainty and opens up a plenitude of cognitive and normative choices. In much of the world, however, many of these choices are religious. Let me connect this insight with the discussion of pluralism in the last chapter. There have been pre-modern cases of pluralism. In the modern world, pluralism has become ubiquitous. Modernity does not necessarily lead to secularization; where it does, this development cannot be assumed but must be explained. Modernity necessarily leads to pluralism. This does indeed present faith with a significant challenge, but it is different from the challenge of secularization.

Let me concretize these propositions with two examples from my own experience. One occurred in Nepal, the other in London. Some years ago, after some lectures in India, I went for a brief vacation in Nepal. I rented a car with an English-speaking driver. We drove around the area of the capital, Kathmandu. One place we visited was a large temple complex, Buddhist or Hindu or both. We strolled around a large platform with a view of the countryside. There appeared to be a commotion at the other end of the platform, with people looking at and pointing toward the sky. My driver was curious and went over to ask what had happened. He came back with a puzzled look on his face. It seems that a young woman, an employee of the temple, said that she had seen Garuda in the sky earlier that morning. (Garuda is the magical bird who, in the Hindu epic of the Ramayana, carries Rama on his back to Sri Lanka in order to rescue his beloved Sita from the clutches of the demon king.) My driver shook his head and said, "I don't think that she saw Garuda." He said it in an ordinary tone of voice, just as he might say, "I don't think this was the morning flight to Delhi; I think it was the flight to Calcutta." In other words, he did not deny the possibility of a supernatural creature flying around in the sky; he just thought that it had not happened that morning.

Also some years ago, I found myself in a hotel in London on a Sunday morning. I am very fond of the Book of Common Prayer; I thought it would be nice to attend a Matins service. I went to the concierge desk, which was staffed by a young man whose nametag said "Warren" and who spoke in an unambiguous working-class English accent. I asked him if he could tell me where there was a nearby Anglican church, and for some reason I added, "Church of England."

He looked at me with astonishment, as if I had asked for the nearest cannibal restaurant. He asked, "Is this sort of like Catholic?" When I replied, "Not quite," he shook his head and said that he would look it up. He scurried around on his computer, then gave me what turned out to be a wrong address. What struck me most at the time was not that the young Englishman was clearly not a regular church attendee; I knew that England is a strongly secularized country. Rather it was striking that he did not even know what the Church of England *was* – quite a measure of secularization. My Nepalese driver, on the other hand, lived in a world in which the appearance of a supernatural being is taken for granted as a general possibility, even if one may question it on a particular occasion. Nepal may well be one of the most religious places in the world, and England may be one of the least religious, but Nepalese supernaturalism represents the worldview of most people in the world today; it is, more or less, the statistical norm, requiring no elaborate explanation. The London concierge represents Eurosecularity, an exception on a global map of religiosity. It is exceptions that have to be explained.

Just before the beginning of the twentieth century Nietzsche wrote his famous declaration of the death of God. It was, I think, as much a prediction about the future of religion as a statement about Nietzsche's own rejection of it. Greater Boston, where I live, has more universities and colleges per square mile than any other place on earth. As a result, we get some sophisticated bumper stickers. I saw the following, of all places, just off Harvard Yard: "Dear Mr.Nietzsche, You are dead. Yours very truly, God." This comes rather close to the empirical reality of our age.

The contemporary world, with a few exceptions, is as intensely religious as any in history. Every major religious tradition not only survives but has generated powerful revival movements. Numerically Christians are still in the lead, with Muslims coming in a strong second. Hinduism is as vital as ever, generating movements that have upset the balance of political power that was established when India became independent. Despite a still nominally Communist government hostile to religion, all sorts of religions are flourishing in China – Buddhism (with troublesome political implications in Tibet), traditional folk religion (most pervasive throughout the country), Taoism (with close links to folk piety), Islam (especially in the northwest, where it has also led to political unrest), and, most dynamic of all, Christianity (much of it charismatic in character). Scholars have long argued whether Confucianism is a religion or a secular system of ethics. I incline to the former view, since the ethical teachings are promulgated against the background of a view of the cosmos that is ultimately religious. Be this as it may, a sort of Confucianism, mixed with nationalism, has become a default substitute for the Marxism to which the regime still pays lip service. Orthodox Judaism has undergone a revival both in Israel and in the United States, with far-reaching political implications in the former. Folk religion of every variety, typically categorized as superstition by the educated classes, flourishes in every part of the world. However, Christianity and Islam are the two major players on the global religious scene.

For obvious reasons, Islam has received more attention. Of course, Muslims are not the only terrorists in the world, but much contemporary religiously defined terrorism describes itself in Islamic terms. The association of Islam with terrorism is, unfortunately, not simply due to Islamophobic prejudice. As a courageous Egyptian writer pointed out, most Muslims are not terrorists, but many terrorists are Muslims. A look at the map gives credence to a phrase used by Samuel Huntington in his controversial book *The Clash of Civilizations and World Order* (1996) – "the bloody frontiers of Islam." Naturally the spread of radical Islamism, much of it violent and aggressively anti-Western, is a matter of serious concern. Nevertheless, it would be a big mistake to simply equate this radicalism with the general resurgence of Islamic faith and piety. From North Africa to Southeast Asia, as well as in the Muslim diaspora in Western countries, millions of people have found comfort and meaning for their lives in Islam. Most of them are averse to violence and have no connection with terrorism. However, many are also conservative in their beliefs and piety, and this can make dialogue with Western modernity complex and challenging. This has important implications for the future, since it is the traditionalists who have the most children. This, incidentally, is true across the religious spectrum: conservative religion correlates positively with fertility. There are many possible reasons for this, which are too complex to address here, but the demographic fact is important everywhere, and it also has political implications.

While Christianity has more adherents than any other religious tradition, it is of course far from monolithic, and its different branches differ in their relations with modernity. Since modernity originated in Europe, until recently the Christian continent *par excellence,* Christianity is perceived in much of the world as a cultural export from the West. This perception can be positive, as a culture to be emulated and assimilated, or negative, as one to be resisted. The former perception is widespread today in China (even within the regime, whose official Marxism is itself a Western cultural product), the latter across the Muslim world. Of course these two perceptions are not mutually exclusive. There have long been voices, especially in Asia, which argued that the "good" parts of Western modernity should be adopted and the "bad" parts rejected. Thus the Meiji Restoration in the second half of the nineteenth century, which modernized Japan in a breathtakingly short period, did so under the slogan, "Revere the Emperor, expel the barbarians!" Japan, the first non-Western nation to do so, rapidly absorbed all the wonders of modern technology and forms of organization but resolutely defended key elements of traditional Japanese culture – including the imperial cult, important portions of the feudal ethic (translated into a value system of industrial capitalism), social hierarchy, and, last but not least, traditional gender relations. Similarly, ideas of selective modernity are widely diffused in developing societies today. The intended synthesis does not always succeed.

The *Atlas of Global Christianity* (Johnson and Ross 2009) provides a very full picture of the world Christian scene. The most important fact is a massive demographic shift of Christianity, from what until very recently was its heartland in Europe and North America to the developing countries of Asia, Africa, and Latin America. There are now more Christians in the latter countries than in the old heartland. As a telling example, more people attend Anglican services in Nigeria than in England. One aspect of this has been instructively highlighted by the spreading schism in the international Anglican communion over issues related to homosexuality, with African bishops thunderously condemning it as a grave sin, while many American Episcopalians favor same-sex marriage and the ordination of sexually active gay clergy. But this particular dispute is only the tip of the iceberg. The underlying reality is that non-Western Christians are much more conservative in their faith and morality than their coreligionists up north. Another way of putting this is that Christianity in the Global South is more overtly supernaturalist, while the faith in the North has made many more concessions to modern naturalism – many miracles over against few, if any, miracles. I will come back to this very important difference.

The Roman Catholic Church can be described as the first global corporation in history. It still spreads over the global scene as no other religious institution does. It claims the most members in gross numbers, though many of those belong only nominally, especially in Europe and Latin America. Eastern Orthodox Christianity has experienced a revival, especially in Russia, though it is not clear how much of this is a genuine popular movement and how much is the result of the nationalist policies of the government. Mainline Protestantism has not done well anywhere, for reasons I cannot go into here. The real explosion has been in Evangelical Protestantism, especially in its Pentecostal or charismatic version; that has been a truly dramatic story.

Charismatic expressions of Christianity have occurred from the beginning of the faith, at the events of Pentecost described in the Book of Acts, and throughout history. As the generic term indicates, these expressions replicate the *charismata*, or "gifts of the Spirit," mentioned in the New Testament – highly emotional worship, glossolalia ("speaking in tongues"), miracles of healing (on occasion including the raising of the dead), exorcisms, and prophecy. However, modern

Pentecostalism began around 1900 CE, a key event being the so-called Azusa Street Revival in 1906, when a black Baptist preacher by the name of William Seymour came from Kansas to Los Angeles and started preaching in an abandoned stable. The above-mentioned charismatic phenomena took place there, to the amusement of some secular journalists who reported on it. They did not have the last laugh. Modern Pentecostalism must be the fastest-growing religious movement in history. The Pew Forum on Religion and Public Life (Washington) operates the most credible ongoing religious nose-counting. A recent estimate is about 600 million Pentecostals (or charismatic Christians; the terms are more or less synonymous) worldwide. My hunch is that this estimate is too low. Much of Pentecostalism is organized in small, local groups, with no phonebook addresses. The estimate is not very reliable for China, where Pentecostalism has been rapidly growing, much of it underground because it is illegal outside the officially registered churches. Most importantly, Charismatic Christianity has been spilling out of its original Evangelical base into officially non-Pentecostal churches, including mainline Protestant as well as Roman Catholic and even Eastern Orthodox congregations. The term "Pentecostalization" has been applied to this intriguing phenomenon. By its very nature, it is difficult to quantify. Let me venture an informed hunch: Most of Christianity in the Global South is at least moderately "Pentecostalized," If my hunch is correct, this is a very important fact, and not only for that part of the world. This is because, as a result of immigration, this form of Christianity is spreading in Europe and North America as well. As yet, it is mainly located in churches catering to immigrants, but inevitably it is attractive to some indigenous Europeans and Americans. Just one example of this will suffice. When I recently returned from giving some lectures in Ireland, I read a local newspaper on the flight home. It contained a story about a Pentecostal mass service in Dublin, attended by about 10,000 worshippers. Most of them were African immigrants, as was the preacher. In his sermon, he said that Ireland was a wonderful country and that he was grateful for being able to live here. He said that he would welcome white Irish people to come to his church. Apparently a few elderly Irish people had already accepted the invitation, as the newspaper reporter mentioned in the story.

For many years the Pentecostal phenomenon was ignored by academia and by the media. The British sociologist David Martin, who has become a sort of dean of Pentecostal studies, thought that people in the educated classes felt uncomfortable with Pentecostalism; he described it as the revolution that was not supposed to happen. The revolution that so many intellectuals *wanted* to happen would come from the Left, not from an underworld of putatively superstitious backwardness. By now the phenomenon has become so huge that it is very hard to ignore. There now exists a cottage industry of Pentecostal studies, with its own journal, *Pneuma* – the ultimate proof of academic respectability. Basically, there are two groups of scholarly interpreters – the "cargo cult" and the "Protestant ethic" schools. The former interpret Pentecostalism as a reiteration of the so-called cargo cult, which flourished in the South Pacific around the beginning of the twentieth century. Some Polynesian prophets announced the imminent coming of ships, which later became planes, that would bring all the technological marvels of modernity – a cargo of radios, telephones, washing machines, and automobiles. The cargo would be distributed to those who had faith in the prophets and, I suppose, who helped support the prophets. Some contemporary Pentecostals, seduced by the "prosperity gospel," also believe that all the rewards of modernity will come to them if only they have faith and give money to a bunch of exploitative preachers. This scenario, of course, is congenial to allegedly enlightened intellectuals. The other interpretation, toward which David Martin inclines, sees Pentecostalism as a revival of what Max Weber classically called the "Protestant ethic," which he saw as an important factor in the genesis of modern capitalism because of its morality of disciplined hard work, abstemiousness and delayed gratification, interest in the education of children, and (last but not least, though Weber himself did not see this) its emphasis on the bourgeois nuclear family. In this interpretation, Pentecostalism is a modernizing force, despite the luxurious supernaturalism that offends intellectuals. My own view is that the two interpretations are both valid. If one is talking about 600 million people, one must assume that these include different types. The quasi-Polynesians are likely to be very much disappointed – I assume that prayer and giving money to preachers will not make you prosperous. However, if you actually follow the morality which the preachers (with whatever degree of sincerity) are promoting, there will very likely be social and economic consequences; hard work, abstemiousness, and so on will not make you rich, but they will get you, and if not you, your children, out of the worst poverty. In other words, the "prosperity gospel" will keep its promise if it is coupled with certain behavioral changes. For that reason, the neo-Puritans are important in a way the other group is not.

Of course this does not mean that neo-Puritan behavior will inevitably lead to positive economic consequences. The overall economic environment can be so bad that no amount of hard work, delayed gratification, and so on will get you anywhere. Alternatively, there may be social or legal discrimination against a particular group of poor people for ethnic or religious reasons, in which case even your best efforts will not succeed. Even so, the "Protestant ethic" is the much better bet than "cargo cult behavior."

If resurgent Islam and exploding Pentecostalism are the two most dynamic phenomena on the global religious scene, the comparison between them is interesting. The differences could not be greater.

The invidious comparison between the Muslim world and the Western countries in any area of modernization has become painfully obvious, especially in science, technology, and the economic development these have engendered. The discrepancy is more glaring in the Arab heartlands, less so in Muslim countries outside that region. Everywhere, however, it has been the source of bitter resentment and anti-Western animus on the part of Muslims. Naturally enough, they have tended to blame Western aggression, from the Crusades to more recent colonialism, including the Zionist incursion into the Middle East. This backwardness in terms of the achievements of modernity is all the more galling since Islamic culture, in centers such as Baghdad or Cairo or Cordoba, produced great advances in science and medicine at a time when Christian Europe was a desert of ignorance in these areas. The decisive turning point came with the Industrial Revolution, which did not even get off the ground in any Muslim country and which made the ascendancy of the West irreversible.

Muslims strongly resent it if culture is brought up as a possible contributing factor to the failure to catch up with the West. That is supposed to be a case of "blaming the victim." It is not necessarily so. Every important historical development has more than one cause. I would stipulate that there is nothing intrinsic to Islam that can be cited as a cause here. If nothing else, the success of some decidedly modern Muslim entrepreneurs in our own time, dramatically so in contemporary Turkey, supports this stipulation. It will always be a matter of Muslim culture *combined with* other causal factors. Be this as it may, there are at least two cultural factors which may be cited here. One is the scope of religious law affecting every aspect of life, including economic activity – a fact inhibiting economic rationality. The other is the role of women. Again, I would stipulate what one often hears from Muslim feminists that the subservience of women is not intrinsic to Islam but is rather something associated with the religion as a result of historical accidents. There is an ideal Islam in which gender equality is religiously legitimated. Marxists used to speak of "real existing socialism" to describe the difference between an ideal socialism and the one existing in the empirical reality of self-described socialist countries. Fair enough; one can also say, whatever one may posit as an ideal Islamic society, that in most "real existing" Muslim countries women are assigned a subservient role both by law and in fact, excluded from economic and political participation, deprived of all but minimal education, and under severe male dominance in the family. These are features that are, to put it mildly, inimical to modern development.

The contrast with Pentecostalism is sharp. This is a religion that could not be farther from legalism – the "gifts of the Spirit" are experienced spontaneously and cannot be encapsulated in legal codes. The relation between God and the individual is direct and personal, without intermediaries. In most regions of Pentecostal penetration, Pentecostalism creates a revolution in relations between men and women. While most preachers are men, women play a leading role in missionary activity and in running the congregation. Very importantly, women are dominant in the family – as David Martin put it, they "domesticate" their husbands. All of this is in the context of the aforementioned "Protestant ethic." That is, of course, a modernizing force in itself, but I would emphasize another point in connection with the Evangelical background from which most of Pentecostalism has emerged: Evangelical Protestantism is one of the major religious traditions in which a personal act of individual decision is at the heart of the faith. One cannot be born as a Christian, one must be born again, having decided (in Evangelical parlance) "to accept Jesus as personal lord and savior." Nothing could be more modern than this principle of individual agency.

It is high time to return to the focus on pluralism. How does the preceding overview of the contemporary religious landscape relate to pluralism? The answer is simple: Religious pluralism has become a global phenomenon.

A simple way of describing globalization is to say that, increasingly, everyone talks to everyone else. It is not only that large numbers of people travel all over the planet, both temporarily as travelers or permanently as migrants; there is also a huge increase in "virtual" conversation, as print and electronic media diffuse knowledge of cultures different from one's own. Religion is no exception to this planetary interaction. In 1910 a large missionary conference in Edinburgh, mostly attended by Protestant delegates from Europe and North America, proclaimed the twentieth-century as an age of worldwide Christian evangelism. It was. Over the last century Christianity has grown enormously throughout the world, to the point where there now are more Christians in the so-called Global South (Latin America, Africa, and Asia) than in the two continents from which the delegates went to the Edinburgh gathering. The Protestant missionary enterprise has succeeded beyond their wildest dreams, especially in the aforementioned Pentecostal version. However, other religions have done their own missionizing. Some of it has been by way of migration from the South to the North, where there are now sizable diasporas of non-Christian religions. Other faiths – Islam, Buddhism, Hinduism, and smaller groups – have also sent missionaries to the West.

A few episodes involving Hinduism, which historically has not been a missionary faith, illustrate this movement. Last year I visited a very big Hindu temple in central Texas, in the heartland of the Bible Belt. A guide said that, on important Hindu holidays, several thousand people come to worship from all over the Southwest. Some years ago I was having lunch in a rooftop restaurant in Vienna overlooking St. Stephen's Cathedral, one of the Gothic masterpieces of Christendom. One could hear some rather incongruous music coming from below. It turned out that a group of Hare Krishnas were dancing and singing in front of the church. About the same time, I was at a party in Germany, where the topic of miracles came up in the conversation. I mentioned the case of an Indian guru, who was reputed to perform rather spectacular miracles. When questioned, I said that I suspected a hoax. One of the individuals at the party, a native-born German, took exception to what I had said. He proudly identified himself as follower of the guru. What all this means is simple: There is an international marketplace of religions. At the very least, the major religious traditions are, as it were, available in a way they have never been before – in books, in the media, and occasionally through representatives present in the flesh. This makes religious pluralism a phenomenon no longer restricted to curious Westerners browsing in the religion sections of better bookstores.

In terms of Asian religions penetrating Western countries, one other aspect should be mentioned. Often without being deliberately identified with specific religious traditions, cultural practices rooted in Asian spirituality have become widespread both in the United States and Europe. The British sociologist Colin Campbell has provided an overview of this development in his book, *The Easternization of the West* (2007). The book is not exactly value-free; Campbell doesn't like what is going on, and a concluding chapter is titled "How the West Was Lost," but this does not change the fact that his overview is useful. While Asian spirituality has made some headway in Europe, the United States has been particularly susceptible. Millions of Americans practice yoga or martial arts, engage in meditation, and believe in reincarnation. Of course people can do yoga to lose weight, meditate to allay anxiety, and learn karate to feel safer coming home at night, but each of these techniques have been associated with religious disciplines of Asian provenance, and the association lingers on in assumptions about the relation of body and mind, of human beings and nature, and the ideal of a good life. I know a young man who has been teaching *tai-chi*, a Chinese mixture of meditation and dance. He is an American with no ethnic Chinese background and is a believing Evangelical. When he proposed teaching a course in an Evangelical college, the dean asked him to meet and questioned him as to whether he could teach *Christian tai-chi*. I first laughed when he told me this story. Then I thought that maybe the dean had a point. Could one engage in Christian prayer while sitting in the lotus position?

Pluralism is usually discussed as a social phenomenon, and so it is. However, there is also a pluralism in the mind. As I argued at some length in the preceding chapter, pluralism has the effect of relativizing worldviews by bringing home the fact that the world can be understood differently. In other words, individuals can no longer take for granted the worldview into which they happened to be born. This insight has vast implications. It was pithily summed up by Pascal as the discovery that what is truth on one side of the Pyrenees is error on the other. No one can choose their parents; neither can they choose the language they first learn. Thus an individual born south of the Pyrenees, in a solidly Catholic village, most likely took for granted that Catholicism was the true religion. Now suppose that this seventeenth-century individual moves north. Not only will they have to learn French, but in doing so they will discover that the world looks different in that language – at least it *feels* different. In terms of religion, they may come across Protestants and agnostics, and even Catholicism is different in the two countries. They may not be very educated; they do not read books; they have never encountered an Enlightenment thinker; but the experience of people who think, believe, and behave differently will start to gnaw at their previously taken-for-granted worldview. A truly terrible possibility looms ahead: They may be forced to reflect – and we know how dangerous this can be! Open one window and the whole turbulence of pluralism may come in. Torquemada, the Great Inquisitor, was quite right about that.

It is possible to conceive of the mind as having several levels – not in the sense of Freud's tripartite system of id, ego, and superego, but in terms of degrees of certainty. The lowest/deepest level is that of unquestioned certainty. The sociological theorist Alfred Schutz (1900 – 1959) called this the "world-taken-for-granted." It is what the sociologists Robert and Helen Lynd, in their classical studies of "Middletown" in the 1920s and 1930s, called "of course statements" – if one asks a question, one's interlocutor will reply "of course." I'll get to some examples in a moment. The next level going up contains cognitive and normative definitions of reality that are widely accepted, so that individuals espousing them are quite secure in doing so and are unlikely to change their minds. Then, going further up, there is the level of preferences and opinions that are held (as Schutz put it) "until further notice" – that is, if given a good argument or a new experience, one might well change one's mind. This relates to an important proposition: As a result of pluralism, religion tends to percolate upward in the consciousness of individuals, from the level of certainty to the level of opinion.

Let me give an example from outside the realm of religion. Suppose that, during the time of the Lynds' community studies, a woman mentions in a conversation that she is married. If she was then asked, "Are you married to a man?" she would have replied, "Of course!" (whether in a tone of puzzlement or irritation). Needless to say, this is no longer taken for granted in the United

States today, at least not in college-educated, upper-middle-class circles. This change is of course reflected in the language – the meaning of words has changed. A few years ago my wife and I were invited to a party where we knew John, the host, but not his sister. Upon arrival we were told to leave our coats in a room on the second floor. I went up first, while my wife stayed to talk to someone we knew. As I got upstairs, there were two women and a little boy in the room. One woman introduced herself: "I am John's sister, this is my partner, and this is our son." Of course I understood the situation, said hello, and went back downstairs. By the time my wife arrived, the little boy had left. When John's sister again introduced herself and her partner, my wife asked, "A partner in what?" The question was perfectly innocent – we know quite a few people in legal or medical partnerships. My wife got an angry look in response to her question, and she was puzzled by this until I could explain the misunderstanding later, since I had seen the two women together with the little boy. John's sister misinterpreted the question, "Partner in what?" as a sarcastic comment. Similar situations are increasingly encountered more frequently and more openly, and consequently less antagonistically, than they were a few years ago. One consequence of this is that the question, "Are you married to a man?" no longer predictably elicits an "of course" statement, as it did in the "Middletown" of the 1920s.

To return to the question of religion, imagine that around 1930 in Muncie, Indiana, the town that the Lynds called "Middletown," an individual said something about going to church. If asked, "Is it a Christian church that you go to?" they very likely would have replied "Of course!" The only non-Christian place of worship that may have been represented in Muncie would have been a synagogue, but I don't think anyone would have referred to it as a "church." Today, in much of the United States, the hegemony of the Christian religion might be affirmed, but as a desired norm rather than a taken-for-granted fact. The American language has come to reflect this pluralistic reality. A quasi-official term is "religious preference," essentially a phrase borrowed from the consumer culture; it implies making a choice from an array of available options. There are also vernacular equivalents. "I happen to be Catholic" seems to refer to an accident of birth rather than a destiny demanding commitment, with the implication that the happenstance might yet be corrected. There is also a more, as it were, Californian variation: "I'm into Buddhism right now," strongly suggesting that I might be "into" something else tomorrow. Survey data on American religion supports this language. A large number of Americans switch from the religion of their parents, either into another religion or into non-affiliation with any religion. The United States, for well-known historical reasons, has been in the vanguard of religious pluralism and has solemnly legitimated religious freedom in the First Amendment to the US Constitution. But religious diversity has become a global phenomenon. There may be some (usually isolated) communities untouched by pluralism, but the number of these is rapidly shrinking as they are invaded by capitalist entrepreneurs, missionaries, and tourists in search of intact cultures. Thus we have Hindu worship services in the Bible Belt, mosques all over Europe, and Protestant missionaries from South Korea braving death in Afghanistan. Why is this?

I have discussed the relativizing effects of pluralism in the first chapter. Let me now introduce a concept from the sociology of knowledge – plausibility structure. I am very fond of this concept. I coined it. If they open me up after my death, they will find it engraved on my heart. What it means is quite simple: A plausibility structure is the social context in which any cognitive or normative definition of reality is plausible. It is plausible in Boston today for a woman to speak of another woman as her spouse; it was not so in Boston a few decades ago. It is definitely not so today in Pakistan, where the implausibility can quickly be ratified by lethal violence. In earlier times, when Rome was less tolerant of other faiths than it has since become, a Catholic principle was *Extra ecclesiam nulla salus* – "There is no salvation outside the church," with no doubt as to *which* church was meant. This proposition could be rephrased in terms of the sociology of knowledge: "There is no plausibility without the appropriate plausibility structure." Put simply, it was easy, indeed almost inevitable, to be a self-assured Catholic in an Austrian mountain village a couple of centuries ago. It is much less easy, and definitely not inevitable, to be so today in Vienna, or for that matter anywhere else in Austria. Paul Zulehner, a Catholic priest who is also a sociologist, has recently written a book about religion in Austria with the title *Verbuntung*. It is hard to translate directly. The German word *bunt* means "colorful;" Zulehner's title means "making more colorful." Religion has indeed become much more "colorful" in most of the world. This has affected the plausibility of every religious tradition. In every tradition, the believing individual finds him- or herself facing the possibility of doubt, on whatever level of sophistication. In pre-modern Islamic thought, in terms coined by one of the leading jurists, the world was divided into two realms, *Dar al-Islam* and *Dar al-harb* – respectively, the "House of Islam," where Muslims ruled, and the "House of War," which was yet to be subjected to Muslim rule. I once met a Sufi poet who translated for me a poem of his about being a Muslim in today's world. The poem mentions the two realms and the border between them and closes with the line, "Today this border runs through the soul of every Muslim." With the proper change in terminology, this poem describes the contemporary situation of a believer in any faith.

Pluralism, by its very nature, multiplies the number of plausibility structures in an individual's social environment. There are differences between environments, some more "cosmopolitan" than others. Even in a society as pluralistic as the United States, there are differences between, say, a small town in Texas and New York City. But nowhere in a modern or even incipiently modernizing society is the individual immune to the corrosive effects of relativization. Thus the management of doubt becomes a problem for every religious tradition. (I have drawn out the implications of this in my book with Anton Zijderveld, mentioned above.) Fundamentalism can be described as a project of eliminating doubt altogether. It can also be described as an attempt to restore, under modern conditions, the taken-for-granted certainty of a pre-modern society. This is hard to do, requiring either a totalitarian regime controlling an entire society, which has very high economic and other costs, or the mini-totalitarianism of a sectarian subculture, which requires constant vigilance against cognitive contaminations coming in from the outside. If individual freedom is posited as a value, this analysis may be called a bit of good news.

Let me make one final point here: Pluralism changes the "how" rather than the "what" of an individual's faith. This becomes very clear if one looks at an individual who has decided to affirm a very conservative version of a particular religion – say, an individual in their twenties or thirties, with a Catholic background with which they never identified very strongly, who now comes to affirm the Catholic faith in a very conservative form. Perhaps they have become a lay affiliate with an organization like Opus Dei. Let us also imagine that this person is a case of what has been called the "third-generation phenomenon" – the grandchildren adopting the beliefs and values of their grandparents, which their parents rejected. Our newly conservative individual is the grandchild of immigrants to the United States from a solidly and more or less homogeneous Catholic community – perhaps from a traditional Austrian village before Zulehner's *Verbuntung*. Now let us make a table with two columns, listing side by side the Catholic beliefs and practices of grandparents and grandchild. Imagine that the two lists are perfectly identical, that is, the "what" of faith has not changed at all. However, the "how" has changed radically. What was previously a destiny, taken for granted, has now become a deliberate choice. The implications of this shift are immense.

Further Reading

Berger, Peter L, Grace Davie, and Effie Fokas. *Religious America, Secular Europe? A Theme and Variations.* Aldershot, England; Burlington, VT: Ashgate, 2008.

Berger, Peter L., ed. *The Desecularization of the World: Resurgent Religion and World Politics.* Grand Rapids: Wm. B. Eerdmans Publishing Company, 1999.

Campbell, Colin. *The Easternization of the West: A Thematic Account of Cultural Change in the Modern Era.* Boulder: Paradigm Publishers, 2007.

Comte, Auguste. *The Catechism of Positive Religion: Or, Summary Exposition of the Universal Religion in Thirteen Systematic Conversations Between a Woman and a Priest of Humanity.* Translated by Richard Congreve. New York: Cambridge University Press, 2009.

Durkheim, Emile. *The Elementary Forms of Religious life.* Translated by Karen E. Fields. New York: Free Press, 1995.

Hefner, Robert W., ed. *Global Pentecostalism in the 21st Century.* Bloomington: Indiana University Press, 2013.

Huntington, Samuel P. *The Clash of Civilizations and the Remaking of World Order.* New York: Simon & Schuster, 1996.

Johnson, Todd, and Kenneth Ross, eds. *Atlas of Global Christianity.* Edinburgh: Edinburgh University Press, 2009.

Kaufmann, Eric. *Shall the Religious Inherit the Earth? Demography and Politics in the Twenty-First Century.* London: Profile Books, 2010.

Lynd, Robert S., and Helen Merrell Lynd. *Middletown in Transition: A Study in Cultural Conflicts.* New York: Harcourt, Brace & Company, 1965.

—. *Middletown: A Study in American Culture.* New York: Harcourt, Brace & Company, 1957.

Martin, David. *A General Theory of Secularization.* New York: Harper & Row, 1978.

—. *On Secularization: Towards a Revised General Theory.* Burlington: Ashgate, 2005.

—. *Tongues of Fire: The Explosion of Protestantism in Latin America.* Cambridge: Blackwell Publishers, 1993.

Prothero, Stephen. *God Is Not One: The Eight Rival Religions That Run the World – and Why Their Differences Matter.* New York: HarperOne, 2010.

Schutz, Alfred. *The Structures of the Life-World.* Translated by Richard M. Zaner and H. Tristram Engelhardt, Jr. Vol. 1. Evanston: Northwestern University Press, 1973.

Spirit and Power: A 10-Country Survey of Pentecostals. Washington, D.C.: Pew Forum on Religion & Public Life, October 2006. http://www.pewforum.org/files/2006/10/pentecostals-08.pdf.

Weber, Max. *From Max Weber: Essays in Sociology.* Edited by H.H. Gerth and C. Wright Mills. New York: Routledge, 2009.

—. *The Protestant Ethic and the Spirit of Capitalism.* Translated by Talcott Parsons. New York: Routledge, 2001.

Chapter 3: Pluralism and Religious Institutions

In the first chapter I used the theory of Arnold Gehlen to delineate the character of institutions. Put simply, an institution is a program of behavior which, if properly internalized, makes the individual act spontaneously and without much if any reflection in the relevant sector of social life. For example, if I sit down for a meal I know exactly how to proceed with the actual task of getting the food into my mouth, to the point where I can completely forget about this task and am able, at the same time, to engage in a sophisticated conversation about sociological theory. I take it for granted, as do my fellow diners, that I will use a spoon to eat the soup, use a knife and fork to cut the meat, will not blow my nose into the napkin or burp loudly or punch an interlocutor with whom I disagree. Of course, I internalized all of these prescriptions and proscriptions long ago – in my case, when as a little boy in Vienna my mother firmly instructed me in the proper bourgeois table manners. Here then is a sector of social life that, by the time I reached an age where I could be taught, had been successfully institutionalized. By the same token, this sector could subsequently be de-institutionalized. Thus, as a young man, I might have come to associate with what my mother would have called "bad company" who regarded sloppy, even swinish behavior at meals as a sign of liberation from bourgeois repression.

Gehlen also uses the term "subjectivization" as a synonym for de-institutionalization. In a well-known line by Emile Durkheim, taken from his classic work *The Rules of Sociological Method*, he instructed us to "consider social facts as things." In French sociology this "thingness" of society has been given the name *choseite*. What is a "thing"? It is *there*, imposing itself as reality, whether we like this or not. Its reality makes it a component of what Alfred Schutz called the-world-taken-for-granted. Yet another term that describes an institution is *objectivity*. In the process of de-institutionalization, this objectivity is dismantled and becomes subjectivized. For better or for worse, I am now free to slurp my soup, eat spinach with my hands, and perhaps physically assault my fellow-diners.

All these considerations apply to religious institutions. They regulate behavior in pious practice until this behavior becomes habitual, taken for granted. A wise tradition in Catholic pastoral care dealt with doubt. The believer with doubts was advised to perform the required actions – kneel, bless oneself, take out one's rosary, say the appropriate prayers – as if one had no doubts, and the doubts would be stilled, perhaps would disappear completely. This advice was wise (and perhaps still is, where pastors continue to give it), because it applied empirically sound insights of sociological theory: All institutions out there in society have an internal correlate in consciousness. Put differently, the objectivity of institutions is transposed into consciousness. This, of course, is what first happens in childhood. The objective institution of proper table manners becomes objective, taken for granted, in the child's own mind. Put in religious terms, the physical good Catholic kneeling in church is replicated by a good little Catholic in the mind of the kneeler.

There is another aspect of religious institutions that is distinctive to them. Once again I can fall back on a distinction made by the classical German sociologist Max Weber, which is, in my opinion, the most useful for the understanding of religion in society – that between "religious virtuosi" and the "religion of the masses." All religions go back to the extraordinary experiences of "virtuosi" – prophets, mystics, shamans – the founder or founders of the religion. These experiences are not shared by the mass of believers and practitioners of the tradition that originated with the extraordinary experiences. The religious institution representing the tradition fulfills two functions: It both recalls and domesticates the extraordinary experiences of the founders.

The contemporary French sociologist Daniele Hervieu-Leger called religion a "chain of memory." Discussing secularization in France, she argued that it broke this chain, and that as a result French Catholic culture has become "a lost world." This may be an over-statement, but the linkage of religion and memory is very useful. The experience of the virtuosi is unavailable to the masses, but the religious institution keeps the memory alive through teachings, rituals, and forms of community. At the same time, the extraordinary character of the original experience is domesticated – defanged, if you will – for the use of ordinary people in their ordinary lives. And that is a good thing; if the original experience were replicated in full by large numbers of people, it would make the ordinary business of society impossible. It is one thing to believe that an angel came visiting many years ago, quite another thing to have him appear every other morning. All the activities that keep a society going would come to seem utterly trivial, as one wants to do nothing except wait for the next angelic visitation. Nobody would want to do the necessary chores of working, raising the kids, voting, policing, or making war.

One of the best historians of religion, Rudolf Otto (1869–1937), undertook a careful description of the core of religious experience or, as he called it, of the "numinous." The basic result of this exploration is that the "numinous" is dangerous. It manifests itself in terrifying disclosures of a reality that is both mysterious and tremendous. There is a wonderful *hadith* (an authoritative tradition) about the Prophet Muhammad on this subject. After the angel Gabriel first spoke to him on Mount Hira and started to reveal the Quran to him, Muhammad was so terrified that he ran from the mountain all the way down to the city of

Mecca, ran into his house, and cried out to his wife Kadijah, "Hide me, hide me, so that he cannot find me again." Kadijah believed in his experience, though she could not share it, and she reassured Muhammad that he was not mad (she is rightly called "the first Muslim"). In subsequent years, Muhammad sufficiently overcame his initial terror so that he could function in ordinary social life, to the point of becoming a head of state and military commander after his move to Medina. We may assume that the memory of the angel never faded. However, for Kadijah and millions of Muslims after her, there has never been an angelic vision at all and therefore there can be no direct memory of it. What was therefore needed was a set of institutions constituting the 'ummah, the community of Muslims – institutions of behavior (morality, law, ritual) and of the mind (prayer, belief) – by which ordinary people could share a "chain of memory" linking them to the great events long ago in far-away Arabia.

Weber is useful again on this point. A centerpiece of his general sociology of religion is the concept of the "routinization of charisma." The term "charisma," as Weber made it into a sociological concept, refers to any extraordinary authority pitted over against tradition or purely rational order. An example of this is when Jesus said repeatedly, "You have heard the scribes and Pharisees say, but I say unto you;" the "but I" claims extraordinary authority on the basis of the unique status bestowed on him by God the Father. The term "routinization" is a felicitous translation of Weber's *Veralltaeglichung* – literally (it would be awful English) "everyday-ization." That is, the extraordinary has become ordinary again, reintegrated into everyday reality. Weber thought that this process is inevitable, probably occurring when the first generation of followers of the original charismatic leader has passed away. The process begins in the second generation, and the novelty has been lost by the third generation, when the movement has become a taken-for-granted institution of everyday life. The routinization of charisma can occur in any movement initiated by a charismatic leader, political as well as religious. The movement then proceeds in one of two directions: it becomes traditional (for example, leadership becomes hereditary) or it becomes legal-rational (for example, leadership is organized in a bureaucracy), a process Weber called a passage from "charisma of person" to "charisma of office." An example of this would be the passage of leadership from an apostle personally appointed by Jesus to a functionary – a priest, bishop, or pope – elected in accordance with precise legal procedures. Only then, of course, can one strictly speak of institutionalization.

Let me give a non-religious example. Quite a few years ago, I had a long conversation with an academic in what was then Yugoslavia. We sat on the balcony of his summer house overlooking the Adriatic Sea. He was telling stories about the time, now some twenty-five years in the past, when he was fighting as a partisan in close proximity to Tito (who, whatever else he was, was certainly a charismatic leader). It was clear from these stories that those years were the highpoint of his youth, not least because of the overwhelming presence of Tito. The ex-partisan's daughter, a teenager, sat with us on the balcony. When I looked over at her, she was half-asleep, obviously bored. She had heard these stories many times before; they held no novelty for her and were part of her ordinary experience. Perhaps she was proud of her father's role in the war, perhaps she was a Yugoslav patriot and felt loyalty to Tito, but this "chain of memory" was a long way from the charismatic fervor of her father. Thus she typifies the process of routinization in the second and third generation.

To return to pluralism, it will be clear by now that pluralism, by undermining the taken-for-grantedness of religion, starts a process of de-institutionalizing it. In Gehlen's terminology, pluralism undermines the objectivity of religion and thereby subjectivizes it. However, this is not the end of the story. The empirical reality is much more complex.

If one wants to understand the effect of pluralism on religion, one should differentiate between the individual and the collective level. As I argued in the preceding chapter, pluralism enables, indeed compels the individual to make choices between different religious and non-religious possibilities. For some individuals, especially if they are philosophically inclined, this may be a liberating experience. For others, it will be painful; deprived of certainty about basic meanings and values, they must put together a worldview from the bits and pieces available in their particular situation. As Arnold Gehlen pointed out in an essay, freedom and alienation are two sides of the same coin. He did not focus on religion, but the point definitely applies to religion in the lives of individuals. The collective correlate of the individual's freedom to choose is the voluntary association – the modern institution *par excellence*. In the strict Gehlenian sense of the term, one should not describe it as an institution at all, because it lacks the taken-for-granted quality of a well-functioning institution, which is by definition non-voluntary. Gehlen used the phrase "secondary institution" to describe this sort of collective entity; it is still an institution of sorts, because it provides programs for individual behavior, but these programs are precariously constructed, vulnerable to sudden changes or even dismantlement. One could describe these formations as "weak institutions" as compared to the "strong institutions" implied in Gehlen's original theory. It is like comparing a toy house put together with Lego pieces to a dollhouse made of steel. This comparison does not imply a value judgment. If freedom and inventiveness are values one holds, one may prefer the Lego house, despite or perhaps even because of its lack of stability.

Many religious institutions have difficulty with religious freedom, especially if they claim to possess divinely revealed truths, and even more so if they once held a monopoly position in a society. The trajectory of the Roman Catholic Church in the modern era is an exceedingly instructive example. I think it is fair to say that pluralism is essentially uncongenial to pre-modern Catholic self-understanding, and that the idea of religious freedom is theologically problematic. The ideal of Christendom precluded religious freedom. The Church possessed the plenitude of truth, and in principle error had no rights. To be sure, the hierarchy of the Church as well as Christian rulers had to make principle yield to practical considerations – for example, in dealing with schismatic or infidel states (such as Eastern Orthodox or Muslim states) or with religious minorities within the borders of Catholic Europe (such as Jews, periodically and when deemed economically useful, or Albigensians, as discussed above). Nevertheless, throughout the Middle Ages there was a degree of congruence between ideal and reality in Latin Christendom. The Protestant Reformation made this increasingly difficult. In the wake of the terrible wars of religion, a sort of armistice was established in parts of Europe at the peace conference of Westphalia, but it did not establish individual freedom of religion on either side of the Catholic/ Protestant divide; *cuius region eius religio* was a political compromise, not a doctrine of religious freedom. The American and French revolutions, both (though in different versions) inspired by the Enlightenment, inaugurated an era in which genuine religious freedom was increasingly realized.

The Roman Catholic Church resisted this development every step of the way, with greater or lesser ferocity depending on circumstances. In the so-called Papal States, which were ruled directly by the Pope and comprised a sizable territory in Italy, this resistance was of course most easily achieved. However, Rome exerted its influence in many different countries, always with the openly stated purpose of restoring its traditional monopoly at the expense of pluralism and religious freedom. The long Pontificate of Pius IX, which lasted from 1846 to 1878, expressed both the high point of the resistance against pluralism and the unmistakable signs of its defeat. Pius IX had begun his career as a theologically moderate figure who then became more and more conservative, a not unusual development in individuals who believe themselves to be Vicars of Christ on earth. In 1864 Pius issued the *Syllabus of Errors*, which amounted to a feisty declaration of war against the modern age and all it stood for. It was a relatively short document containing a list of beliefs and practices that were condemned outright, without supportive arguments. I think that the following two are pivotal. Error 77 condemns the idea that "in the present day it is no longer expedient that the Catholic religion should be held as the only religion of the State, to the exclusion of other forms of worship." Error 80 is the most comprehensive, stating it is an error to think that "the Roman Pontiff can and ought to reconcile himself, and come to terms with progress, liberalism and modern civilization."

In 1869 Pius IX convened the First Vatican Council. It met under very unsettled political circumstances. The troops of the Kingdom of Savoy, under whose monarchy Italy was to be united as a modern and quite secular nation-state, were approaching Rome. They captured it in 1870, depriving the Pope of sovereignty over the Papal States, which were incorporated into the new Italian state. In protest, Pius proclaimed himself to be "a prisoner in the Vatican," a not-quite-accurate description of his status, which was nevertheless the self-designation of the Pope until the concordat with Mussolini, which among other things recognized Vatican City as a sovereign state. Despite the precarious circumstances, Vatican I managed to make two far-reaching decisions, both in defiance of "modern civilization." It proclaimed the doctrine of the Immaculate Conception of Mary, which proclaims that the Virgin Mary was conceived without original sin, and the doctrine of Papal Infallibility, which asserts that the Pope is infallible if he speaks, as Pope, *ex cathedra*, on matters of faith and morals.

The doctrine of Papal infallibility, which has been firmly rejected by non-Roman Christians, is often misunderstood. It does not mean that every statement by a Pope cannot err; the Pope is only infallible in statements about matters of faith and morals, explicitly made *ex cathedra,* from the Pope's throne. Such statements are indeed deemed to be infallible or inerrant. A difficult example of this doctrine, a criticism sometimes made by Protestants with *chutzpah,* is that of Pope Alexander Borgia, who is reputed to have established a harem in the Papal quarters of the Vatican and to have tried to poison the entire College of Cardinals. Would a statement by Pope Alexander be infallible, if pronounced *ex cathedra*, on a matter of faith or morals? Fortunately nothing was farther than faith or morals from Pope Alexander's mind, thus sparing the consciences of later generations of Roman Catholics. This fine distinction was the source of a joke made by Pope Benedict XVI, who has a dry sense of humor. On one occasion he made a speech before officials of the Curia. He said that he was tired and would speak while sitting on a chair (the Latin word "cathedra", in ordinary usage, simply means "chair"). Benedict went on to say that he was not claiming infallibility for what he was about to say.

The decades following Vatican I saw struggles in various countries over these issues that Pius IX had defined very sharply. I think it is fair to say that, step by step, Rome was pressed to modify its rejection of pluralism. Though there is no unanimity on the meaning of the Second Vatican Council (convened in 1962 by John XXIII and closed in 1965 by Paul VI) – many liberal Catholics think it did not go far enough, while many conservative Catholics think that it went too far – it is clear that it dramatically shook up what seemed to be a consensus in 1870. In a tsunami of decrees and documents, Vatican II redefined the relations of the Church to other Christians, to Judaism and the Jewish people, and to other religions, all in the direction of mutual respect and openness. There were other important documents affecting the internal structure of the Church, but as concerns the topic of this chapter, the most important document was *Dignitatis Humanae*, a declaration on religious liberty. It states that freedom of religion, far from being a modern aberration as the *Syllabus* had seen it, was a fundamental right rooted in the dignity of every human being. This constituted a one-hundred-and-eighty-degree turn in the Church's relation to pluralism. From now on, the affirmation of religious liberty by the Church was no longer a reluctant concession to the spirit of the age but a theologically legitimated position rooted in a Christian understanding of humanity. It is interesting that the two theologians most influential in bringing about this development at the Council were John Courtney Murray and Jacques Maritain, respectively from the United States and France, the two mother countries of modern democracy. As the Harvard political scientist Samuel Huntington (who is not himself a Catholic) pointed out, in the years since Vatican II the Roman Catholic Church has been a reliable defender of democracy and human rights, including the right to choose and practice one's religion – a right not just for Catholics, but for everyone, including many whom the Church considers to be in grave error. The new role of the Church as a defender of human rights and liberties became an important factor in multiple transitions to democracy in places as diverse as Eastern Europe, Latin America, and the Philippines.

The last important case where the Roman Catholic Church played its old role as a reactionary opponent of religious freedom and other democratic rights was during the Spanish Civil war in the 1930s and after the establishment of the Franco regime, which for some years maintained Spain as an "integrally Catholic" society. I had an unpleasant experience with this reality in its declining years. As a young man I had been working in Germany, and I took my first trip as a tourist in Spain. At the time I had recently acquired American citizenship. The incident took place in a small town in Andalusia. I had gone for a walk around the central plaza in the early evening. It was pleasantly warm, and I was wearing a summer shirt without a jacket. All at once a Catholic procession entered the plaza, led by a priest carrying the host; perhaps it was during the festival of Corpus Christi. Following the priest was a company of soldiers, carrying rifles mounted with bayonets, their heads bared as they each held their helmets under the left arm. The parade was accompanied musically by a slow drumbeat. It was quite an exhibition of militant faith. All around me people sank to their knees and crossed themselves. I remained standing, in what I thought was an unprovocative posture. No such luck. The entire procession came to a halt in front of me, the priest pointed to me, and two policemen led me away. It was a rather scary moment. The policemen wanted to know who I was. Was I a foreigner? Did I not know that I was in a Catholic country? I told them that I was an American citizen, thus by definition an ignorant foreigner. They wanted to see my *documentos*, which I did not have with me; I had left my passport in the hotel. Consequently I was marched back to the hotel, where my barbarian status was duly verified. The policemen, by then rather mollified, asked me whether I had intended disrespect for the Catholic religion. They were satisfied when I disclaimed such an intention, returned my passport, and left. The hotel clerks were somewhat alarmed by this intrusion of the authority of the state and were clearly relieved when I checked out the following morning.

It turned out to be a trivial incident, though for a moment I thought that the priest would order the soldiers to shoot me on the spot. The reason for describing the incident in some detail is to emphasize that such an event is inconceivable to day, in Spain or in any other Catholic-majority country. Of course this does not mean that all Catholics have fully come to terms with religious pluralism. It does mean that those who have can rely on the teaching authority of the Church for support.

As far as I know, Arnold Gehlen was not especially interested in religion. However, if we explore the matter of voluntary association being the typical social form of religion in a pluralistic situation, we can relate this to Gehlen's theory of institutions. Thus the process leading toward voluntarism can be seen as a form of "de-institutionalization;" a particular religious affirmation is no longer taken for granted but results from a choice or series of choices on the part of individuals. The individual aspect of "de-institutionalization" is "subjectivization." It is a transition from objective fact to subjective decision, which is precisely what Gehlen sees as "secondary institutions" (or, if one prefers, "weak institutions"). It must be strongly emphasized that this does not necessarily imply a pejorative value judgment. It certainly does not if one holds individual freedom as a value. In the spectrum of contemporary American religion, the Unitarians overtly embrace such freedom. They have no agreed-upon creed, rather they describe their enterprise as "a community of seekers." Thus some Unitarians still define themselves as Christians while other Unitarians reject the Christian label. People in more doctrinally focused churches like to make some jokes about this wide-open fellowship. For example, a Unitarian minister once told me the following joke: "What happens when you cross a Unitarian with a Mormon? You get someone who goes from door to door, and doesn't know why." This may be fun, but the joke finally turns on the conservative joke-teller. If you look more closely at the members of most doctrinally defined churches, many of them are "seekers," too. The common formula for this goes something like, "I happen to be Catholic (or Presbyterian, or Mormon), *but....*" The "but" is then followed by a list of items on which the individual differs from the official doctrines of their church. In that sense, most religious people living in modern societies are "seekers."

There is another concept, closely related to the religious history of the United States, which is relevant to the social form of religion as a voluntary association – the concept of "denomination." I have had several occasions thus far to refer to Max Weber (1864–1920), rightly regarded as one of the most important founders of the sociology of religion. Less well known is another German scholar, a Protestant theologian by profession who was also very much interested in sociological issues connected with religion – Ernst Troeltsch (1865–1923). He is best known for his monumental work *The Social Teachings of the Christian Churches* (1912). Weber and Troeltsch were friends; they were engaged in ongoing conversation and influenced each other. One topic on which they collaborated was what they considered the two basic social forms of religion – the "sect" and the "church." They broadly agreed on the basic characteristics of these two entities. The sect is a small, closely integrated group, typically led by a charismatic individual; one usually becomes a member of a sect by deciding to join it. On the other hand, the church is a large community with a diverse constituency, typically administered by non-charismatic leaders; one usually becomes a member by being born into it. Both Weber and Troeltsch agreed that these two religious formations usually occur in a sequence – that is, sects become churches. In Weber's case, the sequence is related to his idea of the "routinization of charisma." Religious movements begin under the leadership of charismatic persons, who lead their sectarian followers out of whatever traditional (non-charismatic) communities they came from. But charisma never lasts. As it wanes, usually in the second and third generations, as discussed above, its authority changes from a charismatic one to either a traditional or a bureaucratic one. As an example of the first type of transition, the authority passes from the charismatic leader to their descendants. More common in recent history is the second case. As a corollary to the passage from "charisma of person" to "charisma of office," as we saw above, Weber followed the church historian Rudolf Sohm in interpreting Christian history in this way: The earliest Christian community, a prototypical sect, was led by the apostles or their immediate followers – charismatic leaders *par excellence*. As the institutional church developed, its authority developed into a "charisma of office." Now the personal qualities of the leader no longer mattered so much; what matters is whether a leader was appointed to office by the proper rational-bureaucratic procedures. Thus the authority of the Roman Pope derives from his office, not his personal qualities. If he was properly elected to the papacy, he will be infallible if he speaks *ex cathedra* as pope on matters of faith or morals, no matter what sort of person he may be. Way down the line from the Pope, every properly ordained priest can administer valid sacraments, including the eucharist, even if privately he is a thoroughly immoral individual or even a non-believer. Thus the "charisma of person" associated with a sect develops into the "charisma of office" associated with a church.

The Weber/Troeltsch typology of sect and church has been debated for close to a century – embraced, modified, and criticized. One of my first exercises as a sociologist of religion was a not terribly exciting effort to modify this typology. The details of this are beyond the scope of this book, but the typology suddenly becomes relevant to our present concern precisely where it breaks down. Weber of course is best known for his seminal essay *The Protestant Ethic and the Spirit of Capitalism*, where he proposed that the Protestant Reformation unintentionally became a causal factor in the genesis of modern capitalism. However, Weber also wrote a less well known but very interesting essay focused on the relation between religion and economic development in the United States, titled *The Protestant Sects and the Spirit of Capitalism*. Particularly interesting for us is Weber's use of the term "sect" in this essay. He uses it in accordance with his own definition, as a religious group which one joins. Yet he manages to describe the bulk of American Protestantism as "sectarian," including the Methodists and the Presbyterians. Throwing these large ecclesial bodies, into which millions of people are indeed born, into the category of "sect" is startling. Something is wrong here. These bodies are clearly churches in the Weber/Troeltsch definition, except for the fact that individuals freely join or leave them. And that fact, of course, is the result of pluralism combined with freedom of religion. The problem with the earlier church/sect typology was taken up in an important work by the church historian Richard Niebuhr (1894-1962), *The Social Sources of Denominationalism* (1929). Niebuhr makes some interesting observations about the relation between religion and class in the United States. But what touches on our concern here is that he usefully modifies the Weber/Troeltsch typology. He argues that it fails to describe the social reality of American religion. Here are churches, not sects, but with one significant addition – they recognize each others' right to exist, *de facto* if not theologically. Niebuhr suggests that we employ a different concept here – that of the denomination. This is a very useful suggestion; as far as I know, the term itself is of American provenance. Interestingly, the term "sectarian" has survived in American English as a synonym for "denominational" – for example, as when an educational or charitable agency defines itself as "non-sectarian," meaning "non-denominational," that is, not affiliated with any particular religious tradition and therefore eligible to receive tax funds without violating the First Amendment.

The denomination as a specifically American social form of religion is clearly the result of American pluralism, and that in turn was the result of the pattern of immigration into the colonies that came to constitute the United States. These immigrants, most of them Protestants, were not inclined toward religious tolerance. Thus the Puritans set up their commonwealth in Massachusetts as a fiercely intolerant Calvinist polity. Dissident Protestants were driven out, and some of them were hanged; but more and more immigrants came into the commonwealth and were unwilling to adhere to the official Puritan monopoly. There was no practical alternative to an ever-widening toleration of diverse religious groups. The situation was very similar in the other English-speaking colonies. At first the tolerance only embraced the different Protestant groupings. Then it kept expanding, to include Catholics, Jews, other religions, non-believers of all sorts, and eventually everyone who did not practice cannibalism or some other criminal atrocity. This development occurred while a political ideology was at hand to legitimate and even to sanctify it – the ideology of the Enlightenment, in its religion-friendly British rather than its secularist French version. Thus the inability of the Anglicans to make their faith the state religion of Virginia happily coincided with the influence of Thomas Jefferson's ideas, which inspired the colonial legislature to establish the first legal guarantee of religious freedom. This does not for a moment imply that Jefferson and others like him were insincere in their devotion to religious liberty, but ideas do not often succeed in history because of their power of persuasion; they rather succeed because they are useful in solving practical problems or serving vested interests.

Over the years, what developed in the United States was an all-embracing denominational system. Sooner or later, happily or reluctantly, every religious tradition in the United States becomes a denomination.

This process came rather easily for most Protestant groups immigrating to America, which were descended from English "Noncomformists" – that is, "free churches" separated from the established Church of England – notably Congregationalists, Methodists, and Baptists. The impulse to set up additional churches separated from the original ones was, as it were, built into their DNA. Anglicans and Lutherans, coming out of European state churches, found it more difficult at first to accept the proliferation of Protestant churches, but in the course of their Americanization they all went through what the sociologist John Murray Cuddihy called "the ordeal of civility" – smiling amicably at people whom their earlier co-religionists defined as odious heretics. Catholics had a more difficult time putting on that distinctively American "Protestant smile," but they were forced to do so as a practical matter long before Vatican II gave them a theological legitimation for it. American Judaism is a particularly interesting case. To accept the denomimational system is to accept the ubiquity of making religious choices. Throughout most of Jewish history, from the earliest times to the emancipation of Jews in many places following the Enlightenment, the idea, let alone the empirical possibility, of choosing to be a Jew would be utterly alien. The one exception may be the relatively brief period in the late Roman Empire when Judaism was a missionary faith. To be a Jew was a fate, not a choice. According to Jewish law, one is a Jew if one had a Jewish mother; one does not choose one's mother, nor (if male) does one choose to be circumcised as an infant. Yet American Judaism has spawned a collection of denominations with truly Protestant exuberance. There are of course the three major groups of Orthodox, Conservative, and Reform Jews, but these are in turn diversified within themselves, and the different ultra-Orthodox and Hasidic groups function as *de facto* denominations. An old joke illustrates this point: An American Jew stranded by himself on an island builds two synagogues – one in which he prays, and one in which he would not want to be found dead. Muslims, Buddhists, and Hindus in the United States have shown a similar tendency to split into different denominations, in addition to being recognized in the larger categories as "sectarian" units in the society-wide denominational system, with the "Abrahamic" Muslims being somewhat ahead of the non-monotheistic faiths, despite the hostility engendered by the outrages of Islamic radicalism. Again the American language reflects this expansion of the list of acceptable denominations – from all Protestants, to all Christians, morphing into communities described as "Judeo-Christian" and, most recently, "Abrahamic" (and so embracing Muslims). There is not yet an adjective embracing Hindus, Buddhists, and Inuit shamans. Just wait!

A denominational system arises when two developments coincide – religious pluralism and religious freedom. One can have one without the other, but religious pluralism is spreading globally even in places where governments want to repress or at least contain it; for example, in Russia and China. Religious freedom, for obvious reasons, intensifies the pluralistic trend. Conversely, I think, pluralization creates pressures toward religious freedom, for practical reasons of maintaining stability if not as an acknowledgment of such freedom as a basic human right. This is not the result of Protestant propaganda or American cultural influences, though Catholic bishops in Latin America and Orthodox bishops in Russia often blame "Protestantization" and "Americanization" for the pluralism that is eating away at their historic hegemonies. Pluralism has become a global phenomenon for reasons intrinsic to modernization, for the reasons described earlier in this book. As a result, American-style denominationalism has shown an unexpected affinity with the conditions of religions in places far removed from its original location.

The Church of England provides another excellent illustration of this development. I will return to this case in the last chapter, because it represents a suggestive version of the separation of church and state (*de facto*, not *de jure*) – suggestive because it may have applications in countries far removed from England. Anglicanism is still today the established state religion, despite the fact that only a small percentage of the white English population attends its services weekly (about 2 %, although the percentage rises significantly if one includes immigrants from Africa and the Caribbean). Bishops of the Church of England sit in the House of Lords. Its Westminster Abbey is the venue of official ceremonies, including coronations performed by the Archbishop of Canterbury. The monarch still holds the title "Defender of the Faith." There is some irony here; the title was bestowed by the Pope on Henry VIII, as a reward for writing a theological tract against Martin Luther and before he broke with Rome over the issue of his divorce, motivated by his presumably non-theological interest in Anne Boleyn. The faith in question clearly means the one held by the Anglican Church, to which every monarch must still belong and of which the monarch is the head. Yet the same Church has become known as a strong advocate of religious pluralism and particularly of the rights of British Muslims. Recently Queen Elizabeth II announced that she saw herself as defending the rights of "all the faiths represented in the United Kingdom," a view also voiced by the penultimate Archbishop of Canterbury in explaining his rationale for the continuing state establishment of the Church of England. The Queen stopped short of changing the title to "Defender of *Faiths*," but this is where she is heading. In that case, she might also call herself "Defender of Pluralism"!

 Pluralism not only changes the character of religious institutions, it also changes their relations to other institutions in society. In this way religion participates in a much wider process unleashed by modernity, that is, institutional differentiation. Most of this is ultimately grounded in the increasing complexity of the division of labor due to modernization. For example, in pre-modern societies just about everything we call education was vested in the institution of kinship, from primary socialization to the various initiations of adulthood. Today we have an elaborate system of education, from childhood to at least middle age ("continuing education"), most of it quite separate from the family. The family could not possibly be in charge of everything from toilet training to the certification of nuclear engineers. Similarly, religion used to be closely enmeshed with other social institutions, kinship again being central. In the lives of many individuals there continues to be an affinity between religion and family, but there is also a large complex of separate religious institutions. Put differently, religion has become differentiated from other institutions with which it overlapped in pre-modern times; religion has withdrawn from many of these other areas of social life. Various sociologists, notably Jose Casanova, have proposed that this differentiation could be seen as one aspect of secularization. It is useful to recall that the term itself derives from Roman Catholic canon law; a building that used to be a church is secularized by being deconsecrated for profane purposes, as is a priest who (with a slightly different terminology) is transitioned to the status of a layman.

Probably the most important differentiation has been between religion and the state. It would be misleading if one simply identified this differentiation with the separation of church and state as laid down by the US and other democratic constitutions. Arguably the institution of the Christian church, sharply differentiated from "what belongs to Caesar," laid the foundation of what occurred in more recent times. Already in the Christian Middle Ages, where the state was itself understood as a divinely appointed authority, a struggle over pre-eminence was waged for several centuries between emperors and popes, between the *Holy* Roman Empire and the separate institution of the *Holy* Apostolic and Catholic Church. The differentiation became much sharper in the wake of the sixteenth-century schism in Western Christendom, when Protestant princes wrested their national churches away from the authority of Rome. The formula *cuius regio eius religio* (he who rules decides the religion) was first proclaimed at the Diet of Augsburg in 1555 and became the basis of the Peace of Westphalia in 1648, which ended the Thirty Years' War between Catholics and Protestants that had depopulated large areas of central Europe. It established the modern understanding of national sovereignty, covering many areas other than religion. Not much later, Hugo Grotius, one of the fathers of modern international law, coined another historic formula – *etsi Deus non daretur* (as if God did not exist). This was to be the foundation of international law, eventually understood as applying to all state law, based only on reason and what Grotius understood to be natural law separate from revealed religion. It is noteworthy that this is was, so to speak, a methodological atheism, not a philosophical atheism. Grotius was a good Protestant, an adherent of the Arminian or Remostrant branch of the Dutch Reformation, for which the Calvinists then in control of the newly independent Netherlands drove him into exile in more tolerant Protestant countries. I will return to Grotius later in this book, because his Latin phrase succinctly describes sectors of society organized by a strictly secular and thus "religion-free" discourse. The Enlightenment was able to build on these developments, legislating religious freedom in various forums, from the First Amendment to the US Constitution to the 1905 separation of church and state in France.

The confluence of two modern developments, the wide diffusion of pluralism as a fact and of religious freedom as a political norm, has by now become a global phenomenon. An argument can be made, on strictly utilitarian grounds, that a measure of religious freedom is a practical necessity under these conditions. This need not take identical forms everywhere. There are significant differences in the regimes of religious freedom even between Western-style democra-

ıs for instance between France, the United States, and the United King-
₋ɔm. A strict separation between religion and the state, as enshrined in the
First Amendment to the US Constitution, is unlikely to appeal to governments
that wish to be inspired by one religious tradition (say, Islam or Russian Orthodoxy) but are still (or so they often claim in international settings) prepared to
guarantee rights to adherents of other traditions. Can a state totally repress religious pluralism? The empirical answer (regrettably) is yes. Saudi Arabia has succeeded thus far, because its indigenous population is small and coddled by the
affluence of an oil-fed economy. With a very different ideology, North Korea has
succeeded because its government is prepared to use any means necessary to
suppress any form of dissent and is indifferent to the human costs of isolation
from the global economy, which requires a certain amount of cross-border communication. Absent vast oil wealth to pacify subjects or totalitarian tyranny to
terrify them, it is more practical to allow them certain zones of freedom. Religion
is an obvious choice for this. The Chinese Communists may be learning this lesson, despite their deep suspicion of religion, a suspicion which is by now probably more Confucian than Marxist.

Pluralism also changes the relations of religious institutions with each other,
broadly speaking in the direction of ecumenical and interfaith tolerance. The so-
called "rational actor" school in the social sciences, originally associated with
the work of Rodney Stark, has introduced concepts of market economics to
the study of religion. As a general perspective on religion, this is questionable.
For instance, a Jihadist contemplating a suicide attack does not sit down and
make a cost-benefit analysis; the passions of religion generally follow a different
rationale. However, when pluralism and religious freedom coincide, there does
emerge a specific sort of market so that economic concepts can be applicable.
Religious freedom deprives religious institutions of earlier monopoly privileges.
Instead, they are forced to compete without recourse to coercion. There will be
pressures toward controlling the competition, which make a degree of coopera-
tion practical. Ecumenism (efforts to control competition, which "rational actor"
theorists might describe as churches violating anti-trust laws, if those existed!)
can be understood as responding to these pressures. In the United States, this
began under the heading of "comity" – agreements between Protestant denominations not to steal members from each other. During my student days, I spent a
summer engaged in this activity. The domestic mission department of what was
then the United Lutheran Church in America (it has since disappeared in two
mergers) commissioned me and another student to do what can be called market
research in a number of communities in the Middle West. Mostly we hit new sub-
urbs. I recall that summer as one of sweating copiously while trudging through
endless new roads, pursued by barking dogs and the questioning looks of suspi-

cious residents. Our instructions were very simple: We were to ask whoever answered the door whether they belonged to a church. If they said yes, we said thank you and moved on. If they said no, we asked them whether they would be interested if a Lutheran church were to open in their community. If the answer to that question was yes, we would take their name and contact information and send these on to ULCA headquarters. Since then "comity" (though the term is no longer used) has come to embrace all faiths this side of human sacrifices, and a high degree of interfaith politeness has become the norm. Furthermore, competition leads to two seemingly opposite processes – standardization and marginal differentiation. In order to reduce the cost of competition and make a broad appeal to customers, products tend to be standardized – hence a decline in sharp denominational differences and a merger of competing entities (cartels). Thus the ULCA of my student comity exercise merged into the LCA (Lutheran Church in America) and then into the ELCA (Evangelical Lutheran Church in America). But there are limits to standardization; if your product is to survive in the market at all, it must have some features that distinguish it from other brands, that is, brand identity. Thus the adjective "Lutheran" has remained – for the time being.

Finally, pluralism changes the relation between clergy and laity. An uncoerced laity inevitably gains power over against religious authorities and clergy. Lay people must be persuaded to become and/or to remain members of a church that is, in fact if not theologically, a voluntary association. They must be relied upon to attend services, to perform the many functions that were traditionally theirs, and last but not least to give financial support, especially if the church has not amassed wealth itself or does not receive continued support from the state. Of course this role of the laity is taken for granted in traditionally "free" churches, such as those deriving from British Nonconformity, but it also becomes a social reality in churches that, theologically, still have difficulty with this, as is the case with the Roman Catholic Church and any other former state church.

The two great effects of pluralism thus go together – faith as based on individual choice rather than on fate or the accident of birth. and faith as institutionalized in the form of the voluntary association. Both have a profound affinity with modernity, which weakens the taken-for-grantedness of all institutions, not only religious ones. Indeed, one crisp description of modernization is that it is a huge shift from destiny to choice in the human condition. It should not be surprising that religion has been greatly affected by this shift.

Further Reading

Casanova, Jose. *Public Religions in the Modern World*. 1st ed. Chicago: University Of Chicago Press, 1994.

Cohen, Charles L., and Ronald M. Numbers, eds. *Gods in America: Religious Pluralism in the United States*. New York: Oxford University Press, 2013.

Cuddihy, John Murray. *Ordeal of Civility: Freud, Marx, Levi-Strauss, and the Jewish Struggle with Modernity*. Boston: Beacon Press, 1987.

Durkheim, Emile. *The Rules of Sociological Method: And Selected Texts on Sociology and Its Method*. Edited by Steven Lukes. Translated by W.D. Halls. New York: Free Press, 1982.

Hervieu-Léger, Danièle. *Religion as a Chain of Memory*. New Brunswick: Rutgers University Press, 2000.

Huntington, Samuel P. *The Third Wave: Democratization in the Late 20th Century*. Norman: University of Oklahoma Press, 1991.

Jakelic, Slavica. *Collectivistic Religions: Religion, Choice, and Identity in Late Modernity*. Burlington: Ashgate Publishing, 2010.

Murray, John Courtney. *Religious Liberty: Catholic Struggles with Pluralism*. Louisville: Westminster John Knox Press, 1993.

Niebuhr, H. Richard. *The Social Sources of Denominationalism*. New York: Henry Holt and Company, 1929.

Noll, Mark A. *A History of Christianity in the United States and Canada*. Grand Rapids: Wm. B. Eerdmans Publishing, 1992.

Otto, Rudolf. *The Idea of the Holy*. Translated by John W. Harvey. New York: Oxford University Press, 1958.

Rico, Herminio. *John Paul II and the Legacy of Dignitatis Humanae*. Washington, D.C.: Georgetown University Press, 2002.

Stark, Rodney, and William Sims Bainbridge. *A Theory of Religion*. New Brunswick: Rutgers University Press, 1996.

Tierney, Brian. *The Crisis of Church and State, 1050–1300*. Toronto: University of Toronto Press, 1992.

Troeltsch, Ernst. *The Social Teaching of the Christian Churches*. Louisville: Westminster John Knox Press, 1992.

Weber, Max. "The Protestant Sects and the Spirit of Capitalism." In *From Max Weber: Essays in Sociology*, edited by H.H. Gerth and C. Wright Mills, 302–322. New York: Routledge, 2009.

Young, Lawrence A., ed. *Rational Choice Theory and Religion: Summary and Assessment*. New York: Routledge, 1997.

Chapter 4: The Secular Discourse

To reiterate my point from an earlier chapter, so-called secularization theory was mistaken in the assumption that modernity necessarily leads to a decline in religion, which is why we need to replace it with a theory of pluralism, a project to which this book aims to make a modest contribution. However, the earlier theory was not completely wrong. Modernity has indeed produced a secular discourse, which enables people to deal with many areas of life without reference to any religious definitions of reality. Charles Taylor, in his massive book *A Secular Age* (2007), has carefully depicted a process in Western civilization by which life can be described and managed without any notions of transcendence. He calls this the "immanent frame." Taylor is a philosopher, and the process he analyzes occurs primarily in the realm of ideas, though he notes that these ideas have affected large populations. This is a perfectly valid way of looking at this history, but it is important to understand that the course of human events is not primarily a history of ideas. To be sure, ideas matter and they do influence events, albeit usually in a simplified, vulgarized form. But the plausibility of ideas is decisively influenced by developments that have nothing to do with ideas but have an affinity with much coarser political and economic interests. To take an important historical example, the Protestant Reformation began with the lonely struggle of a monk with his sense of utter unworthiness before God. The Reformation created an enormous historical change when Luther's ideas not only inspired theologians and preachers but also served to legitimate the hard interests of German princes, such as their interest in expropriating the large real-estate holdings of the monasteries. History is not a philosophical seminar; religious history is not a series of theological disputes.

The origins of the secular discourse are historically complex. Its origins may well go back to what Karl Jaspers (1883–1969) called the "axial age," a period somewhere between the eighth and fifth centuries BCE, when in all major civilizations decisive changes of worldview took place. I think that Eric Voegelin (1905–1985), in his monumental (five volumes) and unfinished work *Order and History*, did a better job than Jaspers in describing these changes as the breakdown of the mythological view of the world that seems to have been the common matrix of all human cultures up to that time. The breakdown was analyzed by Voegelin as a move from "compactness" (reality experienced as one unified whole) to "differentiation" (opening up a gap between transcendence and immanence). While this break occurred elsewhere (notably in India and China, possibly also in Iran), the instances most relevant for Western civilization took place in ancient Israel and ancient Greece, as brilliantly described in the first two volumes of *Order and History*. It is important to understand that these breaks were not exercises in abstract theory but vivid experiences of the world by ordinary people in the relevant societies – by ancient Israelites, who worshipped a God who dwells outside the natural universe, and by ancient Greeks, who experienced the *polis* as an order of reason. Max Weber was also interested in these origins but focused on the distinctive rationality of the modern mind, which gave birth to modern science, which in turn made possible the modern technology that has dramatically transformed the circumstances of life on this planet. Modern science and technology necessarily operate within a discourse that is strictly "immanent" – "as if God did not exist." The immense practical success of this discourse has understandably made it attractive. Let me just cite one basic case in point. In pre-modern societies most children die; in modern or even incipiently modernizing societies most children live into adulthood. It is useful to contemplate for a moment the fundamental transformation of the human condition this fact entails. It makes it easy to understand why the rationality that made the transformation possible has acquired its present prestige.

The secular discourse exists both in the subjective minds of individuals, who have learned to deal with zones of reality without any supernatural presuppositions, and in the objective order of society, in which specific institutions also function without such presuppositions. Thus there are areas of consciousness in which individuals allow the secular discourse to determine their approach – for example, how they cope with sickness. But there are also entire institutions where the secular discourse dominates, exclusively or nearly so – for example, the institution of modern medicine and its local embodiment, the hospital into which the sick individual is admitted. Of course the patient may be visited by a hospital chaplain, allowed in (sometimes reluctantly) by the people in white coats, but it is the latter who are, as it were, the masters of the local reality; the chaplain is a visitor from a foreign country.

As I mentioned in the preceding chapter, the most succinct phrase to describe the secular discourse of modernity was coined over four hundred years ago – by Hugo Grotius (1583 – 1645), the Dutch jurist who was one of the founders of international law. Grotius proposed that this law should be formulated in purely secular terms, without any religious assumptions – *etsi Deus non daretur*, "as if God were not given," that is, "as if God did not exist." At the time there were pressing reasons why any law, in order to be internationally accepted, had necessarily to be framed in theologically neutral terms. Western Christendom had been split into two by the Reformation; there were Catholic and Protestant states, and even the Protestant ones adhered to different versions of the Reformation faith – Lutheran, Calvinist, Arminian, Anglican. What is more, if the new law proposed by Grotius was to be truly international, it had to seek adherence from states adhering to Eastern Christian Orthodoxy (notably the rising power of Russia) and to Islam (notably the Ottoman Empire). Now it is very important to note that, while Grotius' principle at first seems to be atheistic, it was a practical or methodological atheism, by no means an atheism based on a philosophical rejection of religion. Grotius was an Arminian Protestant, specifically an Arminian or Remonstrant, adhering to what I would call the more humane branch of the Dutch Reformation, which rejected the grim Calvinist doctrine of double predestination, according to which God has decided from eternity who will go to heaven and who to hell, regardless of an individual's faith or good works. Grotius was vocally involved in the theological controversies swirling around this dispute, and he was exiled by the Calvinists then in charge of the newly independent Netherlands and died in Lutheran Germany.

Grotius' principle was subsequently applied to domestic as well as international law. While, as far as I know, he did not have such a broad application in mind, Grotius' principle can also be applied beyond the institution of law to the state as such and to entire sectors of society now dominated by the secular discourse; two crucially important examples are the market economy and any organization run as a bureaucracy. Does this mean that all religious discourses are replaced by this secular discourse? It does not. And this is where the old secularization theory went wrong. But the secular discourse inserts itself into the turbulent world of religious pluralism, and this is important to understand.

This brings me to a very important point. If one is to understand the place of religion in the pluralist phenomenon, one must note that there are two pluralisms in evidence here. The first is the pluralism of different religious options co-existing in the same society, with which the earlier chapters of this book are concerned. The second is the pluralism of the secular discourse and the various religious discourses, also co-existing in the same society. For the faith of individuals the implication of this is simple and exceedingly important. For most religious believers faith and secularity are not mutually exclusive modes of attending to reality; it is not a matter of either/or, but rather of both/and. The ability to handle different discourses (to use Alfred Schutz's term, different relevance structures) is an essential trait of a modern person.

Is there a privileged position of the secular discourse in people's minds? Yes, definitely. Is there an exclusive position? In some cases, yes; generally speaking, no. And this is where both secularization theorists and their critics have made a mistake. I first belonged to the first group, then joined the second, but both groups over-estimate the coherence of human consciousness. In the experience of most individuals, secularity and religion are not mutually contradictory. Rather, they co-exist, each pertaining to a specific form of attention to reality. To be sure, there are some individuals who are completely religious or completely secular; for example, a Russian *staretz* who practices the perpetual "Jesus prayer" or a Swedish sociology professor who dismisses every intuition of transcendence as a residual superstition. These two types are perhaps interesting, but they represent a relatively small minority of the world population, with different frequency distributions in different regions of the world.

Two books by American social scientists, both published in 2012, provide rich descriptions of how ordinary religious people manage to straddle religious and secular discourses. Tanya Luhrmann, an anthropologist, is the author of *When God Talks Back*, which reports on a study of an Evangelical group, the Vineyard Fellowship. Its members very methodically cultivate a practice of prayer in which they not only address God (presumably all religious people do that) but also claim to discern when God replies to them. A key concern of this discernment is to be able to differentiate between one's own thoughts accompanying prayer and the genuine voice of God responding to the prayer. Luhrmann makes no epistemological judgments of her own about this claim; as a good ethnographer, she simply describes this in the terms employed by her subjects, without saying whether she thinks the practice is an exercise in illusion. She does, however, compare the alleged dialogue between the Vineyard believers and God with other cases in which individuals converse with interlocutors who are not present in social reality, such as children who talk with dolls or schizophrenics talking with hallucinated persons. One of the more interesting chapters in Luhrmann's book is titled, "Are They Crazy?" In this chapter, she carefully compares the psychiatric criteria for a diagnosis of schizophrenia with the prayer practice of her subjects and concludes that the latter are not crazy. Probably the most important reason for this assessment is that these believers are very conscious of operating with two distinct discourses and try to manage the tensions between them. In other words, the secular discourse is always co-present with the religious one. The two discourses create pressures between them. Thus the faith of these contemporary Americans lacks the calm certainty of pre-modern consciousness and is always tinged with an element of doubt.

The other book, *The God Problem*, is by Robert Wuthnow, one of the most productive sociologists of American religion today. It is based on interviews with a wider sample of contemporary Christians than the sectarian group studied by Luhrmann, but it deals with the same problem, though the conceptual tools of the two authors differ. The question Wuthnow addresses is how self-consciously modern individuals mediate between their faith and the secular discourse to which they are also committed. Wuthnow describes how they manage to adjust tensions between the two in their own minds. The language used by Wuthnow's subjects is interesting. They affirm an essentially supernatural faith, but they reject what they call "weird" or "wacko" forms of it. A telling example of the latter is the episode when a well-known televangelist claimed that his prayer diverted the course of a hurricane headed in his direction. I should add that it is not altogether clear whether the rejection of this particular "weirdness" was due to the authority of scientific meteorology or to moral scruples about asking God to spare oneself and instead to devastate someone down the road. The key issue in both of these books is how modern individuals mediate the tension between these discourses.

The work of Alfred Schutz (1900–1959) was a sustained effort at linking the phenomenology of consciousness with sociological theory. The starting point of the former was the proposition that the consciousness of an individual is not one coherent whole but rather consists of what he called "multiple realities." To explicate this proposition, Schutz coined two concepts – the "paramount reality" and "finite provinces of meaning." The terms are not felicitous; Schutz originally wrote in German, and when, after coming to the United States, he switched to English, there remained a kind of Germanic undertone. However, what the terms designate is clear. The paramount reality is the reality of everyday life; it is paramount because it is the reality we mostly live in, that is, the arena of most of our projects, and (what is sociologically crucial) which we share with most people. Finite provinces of meaning are realities to which we emigrate from the paramount reality. They are finite because they are almost always temporary; we enter them upon leaving the paramount reality, they are real while they last, but they are left behind as we return to our everyday lives. Crossing in either direction, we step across a threshold. Schutz was Viennese, and he liked examples from the world of the theater. So, for example, I am in a theater, waiting for the play to begin. Perhaps I am chatting with a neighbor, gossiping about an acquaintance, or exchanging political opinions. At that point we are still fully in the reality of everyday life. Then the lights are switched off, the curtain goes up, and only the stage is lighted. The play begins. If it is a good play, it will suck me into its reality, which is organized very differently from the reality within which I just conversed with my neighbor. In my everyday world I am in Boston in 2014; in the world of the play I am in England a few hundred years ago. Everything is now different, including the basic categories of space and time. The action in the play goes on for, say, ten years; on my watch only two hours have gone by. Things that I would find completely implausible in Boston today are quite plausible in the England presented by Shakespeare – while the play lasts. After two hours, the last act of the play ends. The curtain goes down, the lights all around me go on, and the reality of my everyday life reasserts itself. Perhaps I resume the conversation with my neighbor, or try to remember where I parked the car, or recall the phone call I want to make when I get home.

Schutz was not interested in religion. The examples he gave for finite provinces of meaning (in addition to the theater) were the realities of other aesthetic experiences (including music), of dreams, of any sort of pure theory (including mathematics). But his concept is very applicable to intense religious experience. This is not the sedate experience of the ordinary believer, which Max Weber called the "religion of the masses". That experience never, or only very weakly, leaves the reality of everyday life; even pious people have been known to gossip or flirt during services. But then there are what Weber called the "religious virtuosi," whose religious experience is much more intense and involves crossing a threshold into another reality. Rudolf Otto, a greatly insightful phenomenologist of religion, called this reality *totaliter aliter*, or "totally other." The great mystics provide prototypes of such an experience. Take a great Catholic mystic like Teresa of Avila (1515 – 1582), who experienced ecstasies in which the everyday world melted away and only God was real. Yet even she could not remain in these ecstasies all the time; they were finite in time, and perhaps also in space – even great mystics may have difficulty being ecstatic in the midst of a marketplace. Teresa was apparently a very competent administrator of the Carmelite convents she directed and reformed, including their finances. Of course the scope of a secular discourse (say, as pertains to financial affairs) was much more limited in sixteenth-century Spain than it is today. Nevertheless, Teresa had to switch realities when she came out of an ecstasy and had to turn to the ledgers of her order of nuns. Even she had to manage the co-existence in her consciousness of her mystical reality and a secular discourse governing the reality of mundane life. Needless to say, this involved a much bigger switch than the one between the fugitive religious intuitions and the ordinary life of the average churchgoer.

Another Schutzian concept, that of relevance structure, is much more applicable to the latter type of religious person. It is important to understand that we live with different relevances all the time, and not only if we navigate between religious and secular ones. For example, imagine I am sitting next to a woman at a political meeting. I strongly disagree with the position of the speaker, and say so. It turns out that my neighbor shares my disagreement. After the meeting we have a discussion with some other people with similar views and assess the chances of preventing the speaker's position from being incorporated into the platform of our political party. The woman I had been sitting next to is particularly passionate in proposing a course of action, at which point I suddenly realize that I find her very attractive. What has happened here? I have switched from a political to an erotic relevance. Of course the opposite switch can occur; a promising flirtation could end abruptly when my interlocutor comes out with political views I find totally unacceptable. It is of course possible that the two relevances co-exist in my consciousness, but I manage to bracket one while I fully attend to the other. In the first instance, I restrain my lustful interest so as not to interfere with the strategic conspiracy; in the second instance, I bracket my politics while pursuing a project classically described as sleeping with the enemy.

When it comes to religion, it is useful to keep in mind that most human beings are not logicians. Thus relevances that may seem totally incompatible to an outsider may not seem so to an individual who is not philosophically inclined. There probably is something like a drive for coherence in the mind, but often this coherence is tenuous or vague. Thus a surprising number of people who claim to believe in the teachings of the Catholic Church also believe in reincarnation or, with more immediate practical effects, practice contraception. Since pluralism means that individuals put together their religious beliefs like a child uses Lego pieces to construct an idiosyncratic edifice, it is not surprising that some of the ensuing constructions look a bit odd.

It should be clearer by now why I contend that the original secularization theory was mistaken in its basic proposition that modernity leads to a decline of religion. It was not as mistaken as its critics believed. Yes, the contemporary world is full of religion; but there is also a very important secular discourse, which has led to religion being replaced by ways of dealing with the world *etsi Deus non daretur*. The modern individual can develop, and in many cases has indeed developed, the capacity to manage both religious and secular definitions of reality, depending on which is directly relevant to the issue at hand. The issue of religion and illness is an important case in point. Probably all religious people pray for deliverance from an illness that has befallen themselves or others they care about. Some believe that their prayer will result in a miracle; this belief is central to the powerful charismatic movements exploding in the world today. Stories about miracles of healing in Pentecostal churches, say about a cancer suddenly disappearing after a healing service, typically contain the phrase that, after looking at an X-ray, "the doctors could not believe what they were seeing." Perhaps most believers do not expect an actual miracle to occur, but they pray that divine power will work with the use of mundane instruments – by the hands of the surgeon or the efficacy of the medication. In doing so, they simultaneously apply both religious and secular definitions of reality to the situation. This differentiation of reality into multiple relevance structures is a key feature of modernity, ultimately grounded in the immensely broad increase in the division of labor. If one wants, one can call this process secularization, but this will imply a more modest understanding of its scope. The capacity to manage different relevances has probably been there from the beginning, ever since our simian ancestors underwent the strange mutation that made them climb down from the trees, adopt an erect posture, and become the species that (rather euphemistically) we call *homo sapiens*. That capacity, however, has been enhanced enormously with the advent of the modern representative of the species, whose *sapientia* differs almost as much from that of Neanderthal human beings as the latter differed from that of a chimpanzee. In the book I wrote quite some years ago with Brigitte Berger and Hansfried Kellner, *The Homeless Mind: Modernization and Consciousness* (1973), we called this modern trait of juggling relevances "multirelationality." I still think that this was a correct insight, which is also applicable to religion in the modern world, but at the time we did not apply the insight to religion.

Religion as one relevance among others? I can see an obvious objection: Does not religion always imply an overall relevance – if you will, a "sacred canopy" – which embraces all the others? Yes, it does. Paul Tillich has pointed to this all-embracing quality through his concept of religion as embodying the "ultimate concern:" What is the ultimate meaning of the universe and all its many realities? However, this does not preclude the mundane concerns that we can attend to while putting the ultimate ones aside for the moment. To do so does not mean that the ultimate – if you will, the cosmic – dimension of all our concerns is diminished or denied. It just means that, right now, we must pay attention to other matters.

Russian intellectuals in the nineteenth century were famous for their passionate discussions of cosmic questions. Yet sometimes they became hungry. There is a revealing anecdote about Vissarion Belinsky (1811–1848), whose short life (he died at age 37 of tuberculosis, the Romantic disease *par excellence)* was spent as a writer and literary critic in St. Petersburg. He liked to have fervent conversations with friends and disciples, often lasting far into the night. During one of these conversations, after midnight, one of the disciples spoke up: "Some of us are getting to be hungry. The food stalls on the street are still open. Perhaps I could go down and bring back something to eat?" Belinsky reacted angrily: "Look, we haven't even decided yet whether God exists. And this one wants to eat!"

I know a very successful surgeon in Boston. He is an observant Orthodox Jew. He expresses his religious commitment in his office, where of course he does not do surgery, by wearing a skullcap; if he does so in the operating room, one cannot see it under the surgical cap he wears there. To my knowledge, he does not discuss religion with his patients; maybe he does if a coreligionist raises the topic, but that cannot happen often. I have no doubt that his religious worldview has shaped the way he understands his vocation – healing as part of the *tikkun olam*, the "repair of the universe," to which all pious Jews are called. I would also assume that the elaborate courtesy and respect with which he treats his patients is grounded in the same worldview and the ethics it commands. I have heard one patient of his refer to him as "a real *mensch*," with no mention of religion. All the same, when he puts on his surgeon's garb and starts working in the operating room, all of this is irrelevant in that situation. Every move he makes, and every thought he has at that moment, occurs "as if God did not exist" – as would happen if he were a Christian, or a Buddhist, or an atheist. His patients, including those who may share his religion, expect no less.

Regardless of the religious tradition with which the secular discourse must negotiate the space for its own relevance structure, there must be the assumption that such a space is available in the first place. If one goes back all the way to the mythological matrix one finds, in principle, no such space at all. Religious meanings and rituals are intertwined with every aspect of human life; what we have come to differentiate as "natural" and "supernatural" continuously interpenetrate. This is what Eric Voegelin meant by "compactness." The same idea was conveyed when nineteenth-century scholars coined the term "animism" to describe archaic religion; the entire world is "animated," full of spirits both benign and malevolent, and these spirits can also penetrate the minds of individuals. This cosmic unity linked human beings with rocks and trees, with animals, and with the gods. Even then, I would think, there were human activities during which pragmatic concerns operated without attention to myth and ritual – say, in figuring out the shape of the best tomahawk for buffalo hunting, even if the weapon was worshipped as divinely animated and inaugurated with the appropriate ceremonies. As I mentioned above, it is possible that this compact cosmos was first disrupted in several regions during the "axial age." In the history of western civilization, the institution of the Christian church was a very important stepping stone toward a secular discourse – an institution separate from the profane world. The very word "secular" derives from Roman Catholic canon law, as discussed above. The idea of natural law, while it originated in pre-Christian Greek thought, became important in Catholic moral theology. It legitimated the application of moral principles accessible to reasoning, independent of the revealed truths of the Christian faith, to large areas of human life. This is important to this day, when the Catholic church asserts that, for example, its teachings on sexuality do not depend on Catholic theological foundations but can and should be accepted by reasonable people adhering to another or no faith. However, the Protestant Reformation was another big step in the formation of the secular discourse. Lutheranism reduced the number of sacraments from seven to two (on the historically rather doubtful ground that Jesus instituted the sacraments of baptism and communion but not the other five), with the significant consequence that marriage was no longer considered to be a sacrament but rather a worldly institution, to be blessed but not created by the church. To illustrate this point, in the early days of the German Reformation there were no church weddings. The marriage was established when the couple began to live together; later, they came to a pastor asking him to bless what had already been consummated by themselves, and this blessing was performed outside the church building. This arrangement changed when Lutheran state churches were established in Germany and Scandinavia, and pastors became in effect officers of government. Lutheran theology insisted on a sharp differentiation between the "Two Kingdoms of Law and Gospel," with only the second being the proper concern of the church. Luther pithily expressed this view when he said that he would rather be governed by a just Turk than by an unjust Christian. The Calvinist branch of the Reformation had much stronger theocratic tendencies, wanting to establish "Christian commonwealths;" but the free churches in the Netherlands, England, and especially North America, with Baptists in the lead, wanted the separation of church and state as a protection for their own free exercise of religion.

Later in this book I will discuss different political strategies for the management of religious pluralism; here I want to emphasize the connection between what takes place in society and what takes place in the mind. A general insight of sociology is that every institution, if it is to function in society, must be internalized in the minds of individuals. The separation of church and state has been the predominant model for managing pluralism in modern states. Typically, it was the demographic reality of different religious groups occupying the same territory that brought about a push toward separation; the practical necessity was then, in one way or another, legitimated theologically. This process is very visible as one looks at the British colonies in North America, even prior to their coming together as an independent republic. The First Amendment to the Constitution of the United States is of course *the* icon of the American separation of church and state. On the whole, while there continue to be tensions between the two phrases in the Amendment's text, that is, between "free exercise" and "no establishment" of religion, it has functioned reasonably well as compared with the often violent disputes between religion and the modern state in other countries. My point here is this: If the First Amendment is to function in the institutions of the polity and the law, there must also be a sort of miniaturized First Amendment in the minds of individual citizens. Put differently, if the secular discourse must be given space in society, it must also be given space in consciousness. That is how religious tolerance has been internalized in American culture, through psychological pluralism interacting with political pluralism. Ordinary American language expresses this fact in conversations about religious as well as other differences, e.g., "You have the right to your own opinion;" "It's a free country;" "Let's agree to disagree on this." President Eisenhower, not famous as a political philosopher, put it perfectly: "I believe in faith, no matter what it is." This sort of vernacular theology is the glue that holds our pluralist society together.

To reiterate this central point, there is nothing mysterious about how human beings manage to navigate between different discourses. The Schutzian category of relevance structure is useful in describing this phenomenon. It applies to many areas of human life, including very directly to the co-existence in the mind of the secular discourse with various religious discourses. This co-existence is of great importance to very large numbers of people in the contemporary world. Thus many Muslims are preoccupied with the question of how to be both a believer and a modern person. In the Christian world, two cases are very instructive in this regard – those of Pentecostalism in the Global South and of Evangelical Protestants in the United States.

I have mentioned earlier the huge phenomenon of Pentecostal expansion over the last century, from a revival in a Los Angeles slum to a population of at least 600 million adherents worldwide. There are different interpretations of the social consequences of this phenomenon in the Global South, where most of it is located. Given the size of the population in question, it is very likely that the different interpretations pertain correctly to different segments of this population, while they do not fit the phenomenon as a whole. After many years of thinking about Pentecostalism, especially in Latin America and in Africa, where our research center at Boston University has conducted field studies, I was persuaded that Pentecostalism must be understood sociologically as a modernizing movement. This has been the thrust of the cross-national work of the British sociologist David Martin, whom I mentioned above. At first this is a counter-intuitive proposition. After all, Pentecostalism proclaims supernaturalism in practices such as possession by the Holy Spirit in the experience of "speaking in tongues," miracles of healing, exorcism, and prophecy. Since Pentecostalism typically first springs up among poor, uneducated people, intellectuals have tended to look down on it as based on ignorance and superstition. I think that this is a distorted view of what goes on. Leaving aside the question of whether the supernatural events alleged by this faith are true or illusionary, the sociologically relevant question is the one about the consequences (intended or unintended) in the actual world. The modernizing consequences of Pentecostalism include the following: Among people whose traditional sources of social support (tribe, caste, extended kinship, clan, village) have broken down, the Pentecostal church offers a supportive community based on voluntary association, the modern social institution *par excellence*. Pentecostalism individuates, along with Evangelical Protestantism as a whole, of which most Pentecostals are a subdivision, and in which an act of individual decision is at the heart of the faith, that is, "accepting Jesus as personal lord and savior." With this affirmation of individual agency comes a sense of self-esteem and self-confidence, which stands out over against the fatalism of much traditional religion. Pentecostalism also fosters the emancipation of women and attention to the education of children, both important factors for the appearance of the so-called nuclear conjugal family, where husband and wife live with only their children in a separate household, which is a distinctive institution of modernity. Brigitte Berger, in several publications, has argued that this form of the family has been a causal factor for modernization. Last but not least, the morality preached in Pentecostal churches is a reiteration of the Protestant ethic, which Max Weber (correctly, I think) interpreted as an important factor in the genesis of modern capitalism – sobriety, marital fidelity, a disciplined work style, and the saving of resources rather than immediate consumption. Needless to say, not all Pentecostals live in accordance with the moral sermons they hear in church; to be sure, neither do members of other faith communities. However, those who do have a significant advantage in escaping from poverty and starting up the ladder of social mobility. The consequences of this can be readily seen in countries such as Brazil, where Pentecostalism has been successful for some time, through the emergence of a Protestant middle class. I cannot here pursue the very interesting question of whether the higher education that accompanies the achievement of middle-class status leads to some modifications of the exuberant supernaturalism of the original faith, but this is certainly an interesting area in which further research is being done. The immediate point here is that speaking in tongues and (supposedly) being miraculously healed does not prevent an individual from being a highly rational businessman; indeed, it may help an individual in this endeavor.

Evangelicals in the United States, especially in the South, are a less dramatic example of a strongly supernaturalist faith co-existing with a secular discourse within which this faith is mostly bracketed. Most American Evangelicals are not Pentecostal, but, certainly in comparison with liberal mainline Protestants, their faith is still robustly supernaturalist. Let me then propose the following, which may also at first appear to be counter-intuitive: It is no accident that the Bible Belt overlaps with the Sun Belt; the most religiously conservative region of the United States overlaps with one of its economically most dynamic ones. To be sure, there are other factors that helped cause the economic ascendance of the South – business-friendly state government, fewer and weaker labor unions, the opening up of the labor market as racial barriers were dismantled, and, last but not least, the ubiquity of air-conditioning. My point here is, quite simply, that the modernization of the economy has not been impeded by what one might call the Baptist hegemony and, to the extent that the latter still propagates the Protestant ethic, could even be helped by it. For the last few years I have been periodically teaching in Texas, and the distinctive Evangelical modifications of the American language resonate in my ears. I will only mention two examples.

"I think we are being told something." This phrase occurs when two events, which an infidel observer might consider to be coincidental, are understood as containing a message from God. Some years ago I attended a conference organized by an Evangelical foundation. The funding for the conference came from a wealthy Evangelical businessman. The purpose of the conference was to consider the possibility of setting up a national Evangelical think-tank; the project was never realized. At the morning session, there was a discussion of possible topics for the agenda of the putative think-tank; somebody brought up environmentalism. In the afternoon, during a discussion that has nothing to do with the agenda, somebody else mentioned the environment. The chairman of the conference, seemingly startled, recalled the fact that this was the second time that the environment had come up, then uttered the aforementioned mantra – "I think we are being told something." He suggested that we should reflect about this and return to the topic the next morning; in the event we didn't. At the time I was struck that here were people meeting in a luxurious modern hotel and looking for signs and omens that would have been taken for granted in classical antiquity. Fortunately no one suggested an examination of the entrails of a sacrificial animal.

The second phrase is: "We will pray over it." More recently I met an Evangelical academic who had been on the faculty of an elite university. He had produced scholarly publications that provided no clue as to his religious beliefs. He was, however, known in the broader Evangelical community, and an Evangelical university offered him a position on its faculty. I don't know what financial or other incentives went with the offer, but he was particularly intrigued by the possibility of working in a decidedly Evangelical milieu. He was at first reluctant to accept the offer. In terms of his academic career, the move would have clearly been a step down. In telling me about this episode, he made use of the other mantra: "My wife and I prayed over it." As a result of this exercise they decided that God wanted them to make the move, and they did. Tanya Luhrmann, in her aforementioned book *When God Talks Back*, describes in great detail the methodology developed by Evangelicals to discern whether, in answer to their prayers, they really hear the voice of God, or whether they are imagining it. In any case, in terms of the topic at issue here, the academic in my story continues to produce professional work "as if God did not exist."

Earlier I referred to Teresa of Avila, who also had to operate in different realities between her ecstatic experiences and the mundane issues of her life as an institutional reformer. However, it is reasonable to assume that, even in her everyday life, the truth of her Catholic faith was taken for granted by her. That is precisely the key difference between a pre-modern society and one shaped by the relativizing dynamic of pluralism. In the latter situation, even passionately asserted convictions have an undertone of doubt. There is always the lingering recollection that one had to decide to affirm the alleged certainties and that other options are in principle available.

As is often the case, an apparently unrelated joke suddenly throws light on a social situation. A young American in search of ultimate truth travels to India. He is told that somewhere in the high Himalayas there is a holy man who knows all the answers to the questions asked by the young man. After an arduous journey to the remotest regions of the country, he finally arrives at his destination. The holy man is sitting in the lotus position in front of the barren cave in which he lives, his eyes fixed on the distant mountain peaks. The young man addresses him: "Sir, my name is Jack Schulze. I come from Cleveland, Ohio. I am in search of the true meaning of life. I am told that you know what it is. Could you please tell me?" There is a long silence. The holy man continues to gaze at the distant mountain peaks. Finally, his gaze still unwavering, he says, "Life is like the lotus flower." Then, slowly, he starts to frown. He looks disturbed. He tears himself away from the distant mountain peaks and turns to the bewildered young man kneeling in front of him: "Do you have any other suggestions?"

As I tried to describe in an earlier chapter, every taken-for-granted definition of reality is relativized by the corrosive insight of pluralism: There are different possibilities of defining reality. I have tried to describe this process in the book co-authored with Anton Zijderveld, *In Praise of Doubt*, as mentioned in previous chapters. In terms of religion, ours is not so much an age of unbelief as an age of doubt. Thus the management of doubt becomes an important task, both for individual believers and for religious institutions.

It should not come as a surprise that the process of relativization triggered by pluralism results in anxiety. There seems to be a need for certainty among human beings, at least certainty about the basic questions of life. Who am I? How should I live? What may I hope for? One should not overestimate the extent or intensity of this anxiety. Most people are not philosophers, and they are capable of pushing away such basic questions and focusing instead on the practical concerns of everyday life. However, the anxiety is widespread enough to guarantee a market for the purveyors of alleged certainties. The latter may be religious or secular in content. In the area of religion, as elsewhere, certainties come in two versions: relativism, which makes a creed out of the uncertainty, and fundamentalism, which purports to restore the sense of certainty. The former is less diffused, precisely because most people are not philosophers and continue to manage the brittleness of all definitions of reality. The core proposition of relativism is that absolute truth either does not exist at all or is chronically inaccessible.

The proposition can come in very sophisticated packages, recently in so-called postmodernist theories, mostly in translations from the French. Long ago the eccentric Christian thinker Simone Weil anticipated these theories when she suggested in the 1940s that people who are hungry may be comforted by the thought that food does not exist in the first place. More precisely, she talked about atheists who, hungry for God, denied not just the existence of God but the very fact of their own hunger. Of course there are much less sophisticated versions of relativism. One should not look down on these; it can be an expression of character for an individual to say, "Leave me alone with your deep questions. I have enough to do, trying to get on decently with the business of supporting my family."

All the same, there are many potential recruits for movements that offer renewed or newly invented certainties. Fundamentalism is a good category under which to subsume all such movements. Some are religious, others not. The alleged certainty may be Christian, Muslim, Hindu, and so on. It may also be political, psychological, aesthetic, even atheist. What all these movements have in common is a project of restoring the taken-for-granted quality of worldviews which pluralism has undermined. Such taken-for-grantedness comes readily in pre-modern societies in which most people grow up and remain in milieus where there is a very high degree of consensus about the basic definition of reality, about question such as, "Who am I?" and so on. A fundamentalist project must then try to restore such a milieu deliberately, whereas in earlier times it came, as it were, naturally. Put differently, fundamentalism seeks to bring about an archaic mindset under modern conditions. There is a more ambitious and also a more modest version of the fundamentalist project; it may target an entire society as a whole, or it may limit its ambition to a segment of society, to a subculture or sect. Both are difficult, because both require keeping out the powerful effects of pluralism. The more ambitious fundamentalism implies some sort of totalitarian regime, which controls all or at least most communications that contradict the official worldview. Unless the regime has successfully suppressed all channels of dissident communication, and unless it can cut itself off from the world economy, which depends on a high degree of open communication, it is difficult to impose on a modern society a culture that is, essentially, archaic. Domestically, contemporary media of communication tend to escape from total control. In relations with the outside world, high economic and human costs are incurred by cutting off or even strictly limiting interaction with the world economy. Currently North Korea is one of the few examples of a regime that has set up a highly successful (thus far) system of repression and has been indifferent to the human costs of its economic policies. The history of totalitarian experiments thus far does not suggest an optimistic prognosis for the long-term survival of such regimes, which, I suppose, falls under the heading of good news.

Both relativism and fundamentalism are dangerous for individuals and much more so for society. Relativism moves individuals toward moral nihilism, fundamentalism toward fanaticism. Neither is attractive as a way of life, but as long as my nihilistic or fanatical neighbors do not seek to impose their views on me, I can live with them and collaborate in taking out the trash. However, the threat to society is harder to manage. If there is no agreement at all on what is permissible behavior (in Emile Durkheim's phrase, no "collective conscience"), the moral basis and consequently the very existence of a society is put in question. It will lack the solidarity that motivates individuals to make sacrifices for fellow members of the society and ultimately motivates them to risk their lives if the society is attacked. Fundamentalism, even if it is not successful in imposing itself on the entire society (with the abovementioned ensuing costs), will bring about ongoing conflict which, even short of civil war, will undermine social stability.

Let me recall Arnold Gehlen's theory of institutions, which I discussed earlier in this book. The theory suggests that institutions function best when they resemble instincts – programs of behavior that can be followed spontaneously, without reflection. That is, strong institutions are taken for granted by individuals who have been socialized into them. Modern pluralism undermines this taken-for-grantedness, forcing individuals to hesitate and reflect about the institutional programs. Helmut Schelsky, a German sociologist influenced by Gehlen, has coined the term *Dauerreflektion* ("permanent reflection") to describe this process. Conservatives, by the way, have always known this; too much thinking is bad for social stability, therefore intellectuals are plausible targets for police surveillance.

Once again, an old joke nicely illustrates this insight. The friend of a man with a long beard asks him, "Tell me, when you go to bed, do you keep your beard above or below the blanket?" The bearded man admits that he never thought about this, doesn't know the answer, and will now pay attention. A few days later they meet again. The man with the beard is very angry. "Since our conversation I haven't been able to sleep. I keep awake, watching where my beard ends up."

Thus doubt is the pivot around which the dynamics of pluralism whirl. In the mind, doubt almost always accompanies faith – maybe not for Weber's "religious virtuosi" but for the great majority of ordinary believers. This does not mean that the latter cannot have strong convictions, but these very likely will lack the relaxed certitude of pre-modern people. In society, the management of doubt means that dissent from the official definitions of reality must somehow be contained. If the authorities are reluctant or unwilling to squash all dissent, they must find ways to co-exist with it. Religious freedom can be limited or general. However, quite apart from its intrinsic worth, a measure of religious freedom becomes a political imperative.

Further Reading

Berger, Peter L, Brigitte Berger, and Hansfried Kellner. *The Homeless Mind: Modernization and Consciousness.* New York: Random House, 1973.

Berger, Peter L., ed. *Between Relativism and Fundamentalism: Religious Resources for a Middle Position.* Grand Rapids: Wm. B. Eerdmans Publishing, 2010.

Casanova, Jose. "The Secular, Secularizations, Secularisms." In *Rethinking Secularism*, edited by Craig Calhoun, Mark Juergensmeyer, and Jonathan VanAntwerpen, 54–74. New York: Oxford University Press, 2011.

Cox, R. R. *Schutz's Theory of Relevance: A Phenomenological Critique.* The Hague: Martinus Nijhoff, 1978.

Jaspers, Karl. *The Origin and Goal of History.* New Haven: Yale University Press, 1953.

Juergensmeyer, Mark. *Global Rebellion: Religious Challenges to the Secular State, from Christian Militias to Al Qaeda.* Berkeley: University of California Press, 2008.

—. "Rethinking the Secular and Religious Aspects of Violence." In *Rethinking Secularism*, edited by Craig Calhoun, Mark Juergensmeyer, and Jonathan VanAntwerpen, 185–203. New York: Oxford University Press, 2011.

Luhrmann, Tanya M. *When God Talks Back: Understanding the American Evangelical Relationship with God.* New York: Alfred A. Knopf, 2012.

Martin, David. "Another Kind of Cultural Revolution?" In *Faith on the Move: Pentecostalism and Its Potential Contribution to Development*, edited by Roger Southall and Stephen Rule, 7–19. Johannesburg: Centre for Development and Enterprise, 2008.

McCoubrey, Hilaire. "Natural Law, Religion and the Development of International Law." In *Religion and International Law*, edited by Mark W. Janis and Carolyn Maree Evans, 177–190. The Hague: Martinus Nijhoff Publishers, 1999.

Schuetz, Alfred. "On Multiple Realities." *Philosophy and Phenomenological Research* 5, no. 4 (June 1, 1945): 533–576.

Taylor, Charles. *A Secular Age.* Cambridge: Harvard University Press, 2007.

Tuck, Richard. *Natural Rights Theories: Their Origin and Development.* New York: Cambridge University Press, 1998.

Voegelin, Eric. *Order and History.* Vol. 1–2. 34 vols. The Collected Works of Eric Voegelin 14–15. Columbia: University of Missouri Press, 2000.

Wuthnow, Robert. *The God Problem: Expressing Faith and Being Reasonable.* Los Angeles: University of California Press, 2012.

Chapter 5: Religion and Multiple Modernities

The late Israeli sociologist Shmuel Eisenstadt (1923–2010) made a very useful contribution to the topic of this book, though like Alfred Schutz he was, as far as I know, not particularly interested in religion. In a 2000 article in the journal *Daedalus*, he proposed the concept of "multiple modernities," which attracted widespread attention and which he elaborated further in some later publications. It is, I think, an important contribution to our understanding of modernity, and it is very applicable to the relation secularity and religion in modern societies. The central idea here is quite simple: Modernity does not come in one version only, but in several versions. After World War II, when many social scientists sought to understand the processes of modernization which were radically transforming what was then called the Third World (that is, the countries of Asia, Africa, and Latin America), the prevailing notion was that modernity came in one version only – that of Western civilization. Some were quite happy with this, among them Talcott Parsons, who at that time was a sort of maharaja of American sociology; Eisenstadt had been his student at Harvard. Others deplored the alleged fact, looking upon it as an expression of Western imperialism and cultural homogenization. Eisenstadt's concept challenged a key assumption of the then-dominant understanding of modernization, dampening the enthusiasm of some as well as the apprehensions of others.

I have given the name "electric toothbrush theory of modernization" to the idea that modernity comes in one version only. This idea implies that if one drops an electric toothbrush into the Amazonian rainforest, within one generation the place will look like Cleveland. The idea is not completely crazy. For example, the simple introduction of cell phones into rural Africa has dramatically changed the lives of local farmers, as has the introduction of basic practices of modern medicine, even if these intrusions of modernity are very circumscribed, leaving most traditional culture undisturbed. Nevertheless, even larger importations of modern technology do not necessarily lead to overall Westernization.

An example of multiple modernities in action can be taken from another encounter involving cell phones. On one of my early visits to Hong Kong, I went for a walk. I came upon a Buddhist temple and stepped inside. What I saw was remarkable. In front of a large statue of the Buddha stood a middle-aged Chinese man in a business suit, bowed in a posture of devotion. In one hand he held an incense stick, in the other hand a cell phone into which he was speaking. My first thought was: Just who is he talking to? Clearly, I was then fully in the paramount reality of a tourist excursion – definitely in the grip of the secular discourse, just as I am now, while writing this book – a definitely secular exercise of developing an argument as a sociologist. Hence, then and now, I did not and will not entertain the notion that this man was talking to a supernatural being, such as one of the many Boddhisatvas to whom one may pray for help in the journey toward enlightenment. I did recall then, and I am recalling now, that Overseas Chinese (including those residing in Hong Kong) are one of the most economically successful groups of people in the world. Indeed, I was in Hong Kong visiting a research project on the economic culture of Overseas Chinese entrepreneurs, which our research center at Boston University conducted under the direction of Gordon Redding, who was dean of the business school at the University of Hong Kong at that time. *Ergo* I assumed then, and will assume now, that the man in the temple was not engaging in conversation with the beyond, but rather conversing with human beings. This conversation could have had to do with any number of areas of the man's life, and may perhaps have been in the context of some business transaction. Chinese entrepreneurs are a thoroughly pragmatic bunch, even in their attitudes toward religion. Nevertheless, at this moment the man was simultaneously performing an act of worship (bowing with an incense stick in hand) *and* engaging in a mundane conversation (that was and is my very secular assumption). In retrospect, I regret that we could not interview this individual as part of our research project. I would love to know how he managed to balance his religious and business relevance structures. While physically engaged in an act of Buddhist worship, he was also simultaneously engaged in what is usually a secular form of communication. He certainly seemed quite successful in managing this synthesis.

Sometime in the 1920s King Ibn Saud, the founder of the Saudi Arabian state, wanted to install a telephone line between Riadh, the capital in the interior, and Jeddah, the port city on the Red Sea. The Muslim clerics in his entourage were strongly opposed to this. They maintained that the telephone was a satanic instrument. Thereupon the king arranged for passages of the Quran to be read over the telephone, demonstrating that it could not be a satanic instrument because the sacred text could be carried by it. Since then, of course, Saudi Arabia has absorbed an impressive emporium of modern technology, which has not prevented its operating under a deeply conservative form of *sharia* law, including what appear to Westerners as profoundly offensive civil and criminal provisions. One may also note that the Islamic revolution in Iran was inspired by sermons of the Ayatollah Khomeini smuggled in from his foreign exile on audio cassettes, and that Jihadist terror groups use the Internet to spread their message and gain recruits.

Japan is a centrally important case for any discussion of multiple modernities. Eisenstadt was very interested in it and wrote a book devoted to the subject. Japan was the first non-Western country to modernize very fully, and it did so in an amazingly short period of time. Yet to this day, despite all sorts of changes due to global influences, Japan has retained a distinctively non-Western culture. Anyone arriving at Narita airport and going on from there for even a brief sojourn in the country can have direct experience of this fact. One's first impressions are of a thoroughly modern culture, in some respects more modern than that of any country in Europe or North America, beginning with the posted schedule of buses from Narita to downtown Tokyo, showing departure times broken down in precise minutes – a schedule which, at least in my experience, is amazingly accurate; even Swiss railways cannot compete. Yet one need not stay in Japan for very long to realize that here is a culture still very different from anything one is familiar with in Cleveland or Düsseldorf.

The so-called Meiji Restoration of 1868, which inaugurated Japan's extraordinary modernization process, overthrew the Shogunate, the feudal regime that had kept the country carefully isolated from all but the most controlled foreign influences. It supposedly restored the power of the Emperor, though actually the government was in the hands of a group of oligarchs drawn from the old aristocracy. It was concern over foreign intervention that triggered their rebellion. In 1854 Commodore Perry of the US Navy sailed his flotilla into Tokyo Bay and forced the Shogun government to open up to foreign trade. The government gave in almost immediately. What took place in the fourteen years that followed was a process of intensive reflection within the Japanese elite, dominated by one thought – how to avoid the fate of China, which had become the object of prolonged imperialist penetration and exploitation by Western powers, virtually abolishing it as a sovereign state; the most odious expression of this was the Opium War, in which Britain forced China to allow the importation of opium in the name of free trade. The slogan of the Meiji rebels was, "Revere the Emperor, expel the barbarians." To accomplish this, the Meiji regime adopted a large package of "barbarian" technologies and institutions, but with the purpose of making Japan into a modern state capable of asserting its power internationally and defending the core values of its culture. The feudal ethos was universalized; not just the Samurai class but all citizens were indoctrinated in an ethic of loyalty to superiors in a renovated hierarchy, first of all to the Emperor, the symbol of national unity, but also, and with enormous economic consequences, to the capitalist firms that sprang up following the dismantling of the feudal system. Shintoism, which had always co-existed with Buddhism as an indigenous folk religion, was elevated into an obligatory political cult, devoted to celebrating the divine status of the Emperor. All feudal ranks were abolished, all citizens were equal before the law, and universal public education was instituted, at first beginning with elementary school, to create an educated labor force. The state made sure that the basic technological infrastructure of a modern society (railways, telecommunications, an electricity grid) was quickly put into place. Very importantly, the military was rapidly modernized. The speed with which all of this happened was breathtaking. By 1905 it had reached the point where Japan was able to defeat Russia, one of the great European powers, on land and on the sea.

The Meiji oligarchs were a remarkably reflective group of people. Early in the process of revamping the country, they sent a large delegation to visit the major Western countries – the United States, Britain, France, and Germany. The express purpose of the mission was to find out which items of Western civilization Japan should adopt and, just as importantly, which it should reject. The mission took many months, but it came back with very specific recommendations. They were not much impressed with Western democracy, but they liked American and British engineering. They also liked the capitalist market economy and some aspects of French civil law. Best of all they liked Germany, where Bismarck received them very cordially. He advised them to have some sort of parliament, because that was expected of a modern country, but they should make sure that its powers were limited; real power should remain in the hands of the monarch and those acting on his behalf. They certainly followed that advice! It is difficult to think of other cases in history in which a fundamental transformation of a society was achieved with such an exercise of rational reflection and planning.

The project of the Meiji Restoration was successful beyond the wildest dreams of its initiators. For a long time, many traits of pre-modern Japanese culture survived the modernization process, including, which is important for the argument of this book, its religious components of Buddhism (with a variety of schools), Shintoism (though deprived of its political status after 1945), and Confucian-inspired ethics. Interestingly, in the post-World-War-II era Japan has shown itself quite immune to the inroads of Christianity, in sharp contrast with Korea, China, and the Chinese diaspora. Japan continues to be a deeply hierarchical culture, despite the successful adoption of democracy since the American occupation. Traditional values of gender and age remained intact for much of this period, as well as a generally collectivistic orientation as over against an individualistic one. Of course the culture has changed. It is now less deferential, less collectivistic, more egalitarian, and more permissive in gender relations. No place in Japan has become quite like Cleveland, millions of electric toothbrushes notwithstanding. Eisenstadt was right in giving Japan pride of place in his catalogue of multiple modernities.

Imagine a pilot of Japan Airlines. While he flies the plane from the cockpit, both his conscious attention and his behavior are rigorously standardized. These standards are exactly the same regardless of the nationality of the pilot or his airline. What is more, the standards conform completely to a distinctively modern discourse, certainly completely separated from any religious discourse. The situation is very different once the plane has landed and the pilot leaves the cockpit and goes home. Then imagine that the pilot is a very conservative individual; there are such in many occupations in Japan. It may then be imagined that his private life is dominated by values and behavior patterns that are rooted in pre-modern Japanese culture – in terms of his relations to his wife and his children as well as to his and his wife's parents, his loyalties to different echelons in the social hierarchy, his views on any number of political issues, and, last but not least, in terms of religion. Perhaps, as soon as our pilot comes home and has changed into traditional clothing, he will sit before a little Buddhist shrine in the apartment and chant sutras or engage in meditation.

This suggests a metaphor, a visual discrimination between inside the cockpit and outside the cockpit. I will shortly elaborate the metaphor conceptually. The story does not necessarily involve religion, but it is very relevant to the topic of this chapter, that is, the pluralism of secular and religious discourses. Let me expand the scope of my imagination for a moment. Imagine the Pope traveling in the (presumably exclusive) cabin of the Japanese plane. Even imagine him celebrating Mass in flight. He should have no trouble executing this feat, unless he is interrupted by sudden turbulence. However, I daresay he would not want the pilot to practice Zen meditation in the cockpit, or, for that matter, to have an authentically Catholic mystic experience.

Running an airline involves at least three very important discourses, each based on a strictly secular relevance structure, "as if God did not exist" – the discourse of technology, the discourse of bureaucracy, and (in most cases today) the discourse of the capitalist market economy. It is not only the pilot who must, while on the job, bracket whatever religious beliefs or values he may have; so must the government official regulating air traffic and the investment broker who is concerned with the standing of airline shares on the stock exchange. These discourses are very powerful in a modern society, and they exert pressure on religion. Their distinctive logic frequently invades the religious discourse itself. Thus clergy and ordinary believers may look on their religion in terms derived from allegedly scientific medicine – as fostering mental or even physical health or improving intimate relationships – and technical methods will be devised to achieve these secular goals. Thus religious organizations will modernize themselves by instituting bureaucratic structures, which often modify or even replace the original religious principles of churches; denominational headquarters may look much like those of government or corporate offices, with their functionaries thinking in terms of the productivity and efficient deployment of "human resources." And the secular logic of capitalism may invade the way people think about religion, in terms of costs and benefits, returns on investment, and the like (as in the "rational actor" school of the sociology of religion, mentioned above, which seeks to analyze all religious phenomena by using such categories). These empirical realities indicate where the old secularization theory was not altogether wrong. Nevertheless, their pressures did not replace religious discourses, not even when reinforced by often violent coercion, as in most Communist states. Regardless of the massive diffusion of electric toothbrushes, the gods refused to go away. On the contrary, in most of the contemporary world they flourish as never before. Taylor's *A Secular Age* provides a detailed picture of the secular discourse or "immanent frame" that has become very important in the modern world. However, the title of the book is misleading. The phrase "secular age" hardly describes the empirical state of affairs in most of the contemporary world. The key proposition of this book is that our age would best be described as pluralist rather than secular.

I have previously mentioned the book *The Homeless Mind: Modernization and Consciousness* (1973), which I co-authored with Brigitte Berger and Hansfried Kellner. While there are some things I would put differently now, I think the basic approach of linking distinctively modern forms of consciousness with their institutional correlates (among them, prominently, technology and bureaucracy) continues to be valid. At the time, we were not focused on religion. We began work on the book in Mexico, while associated with Ivan Illich's idiosyncratic think-tank in Cuernavaca. Almost all of our Mexican interlocutors were Marxists of one variety or another, who ascribed all features of modernization (which they defined as negative features) to the cultural effects of capitalist imperialism. Against this Marxist consensus, we wanted to show that certain basic features of modernity were there, no matter whether the economy was organized along capitalist or socialist lines. The global collapse of socialism has made this focus less interesting today, but some of the concepts we developed then are quite applicable to the topic of the co-existence of secular and religious discourses.

In the book, we distinguished between what we called "intrinsic and extrinsic packages." A package is a specific linkage between items of consciousness and behavior. An intrinsic package is one that cannot be taken apart if a particular action is to succeed. An extrinsic package is one that can be taken apart and re-assembled in a different way, without the action failing. To return to the previous metaphor, a pilot must be trained to operate with a very specific package of consciousness and behavior while functioning in the cockpit – for example, to be able to correlate precisely every action with the readings on the screen regarding altitude, speed, fuel consumption, and so on. This package is intrinsic; if the pilot has not successfully internalized this package, the plane will crash. However, at least if he flies on international routes, the pilot will also have to learn English, since that is the language used worldwide in communications with air traffic controllers. The English language is now part of the package that has to be learned by any individual training to be a pilot in international aviation. That package linking habits of precision and command of English is extrinsic; it came about because of the early economic dominance of the United States in the field of air travel. In principle, any other language capable of handling the required technical terminology could be substituted for English.

It will be clear from the preceding chapters that the intrinsic packages of modernity will be under the sway of the secular discourse. Extrinsic packages, by definition, are much more variegated. In the early 1970s, when we were working on *The Homeless Mind* as a cognitive minority amid the cacophony of Marxist voices, we were right in insisting that certain features of modernity are intrinsic, no matter whether a society is organized on capitalist or socialist lines, except that socialism today is much less plausible as an alternative. Religious discourses, in many different versions, are very much present as extrinsic items in packages of modernity. To say this in no way denigrates their importance. For anyone whose faith provides the ultimate meaning of their life, the religious component of the package with which they operate in life will be more important than any other component, no matter that the latter is more intrinsic than their faith to the functioning of a modern society.

Once the secular discourse has been established, both in the minds of individuals and in society, it is inevitable that there will be boundary disputes. Radical secularists, whose worldview has been philosophically legitimated ever since the Enlightenment, will deny that there is a problem of boundaries. Rational thought, as they understand it, is the only valid form of knowledge; every other discourse, including such as is at the center of most religions, is superstition to be denounced and ejected from the accepted cognitive canon. There are no boundaries to be negotiated, because "error has no rights" – certainly no right to a separate relevance structure whose boundaries are to be respected. A current example of this is the effort by some determined atheists to explain, and *ipso facto* to explain away, all religious phenomena in terms of neurology; God is nothing but a twitching in some part of the human brain.

On the other side of the epistemological divide, there have been attempts to portray religion itself as a science. Given the prestige of science and its power to transform human life, this is quite understandable. In American religious history, a prototype of this kind of exercise is Christian Science, founded by Mary Baker Eddy (1821–1910). In her major work, *Science and Health, With Key to the Scriptures,* she presented "Christ, Scientist" as the teacher of a scientific methodology that can lead to spiritual and physical health. She must have been a remarkable woman, who succeeded in basing an entire new denomination on her rather bizarre interpretation of Christianity. While Christian Science never became an influential entity in American religion, the denomination survives to this day. Its impressive Mother Church still features on the Boston skyline, and its newspaper, the *Christian Science Monitor,* is a widely respected publication (partly, I suspect, because it underplays the denomination's theology).

On a higher level of sophistication is the movement of Anthroposophy, founded by the eccentric Austrian genius Rudolf Steiner (1861–1925). Steiner was a prolific writer, but arguably his seminal work was *How to Know Higher Worlds: A Modern Path to Initiation.* He proposed that a "spiritual science," as he understood it, could open up the supernatural world to a mind that does not therefore abandon modern rationality. In addition to the Anthroposophical Society, which is devoted to the study and practice of his teachings, Steiner created an innovative educational movement (the Waldorf Schools, known as Steiner Schools in the United States) with distinctive approaches to medicine, architecture, and art. He also founded a separate church, the Christian Community (*Christengemeinschaft*), which celebrates a sacrament (the so-called *Menschenweihehandlung)* and is as close as one can get today to an archaic mystery cult. Incidentally, a truly startling cultic language is used in this ritual, with the potential of catapulting an innocent visitor into a "totally other" reality. The Anthroposophical community is small, but it has branches in several countries and has had a particular appeal to people in the natural sciences.

A recent controversy in the United States has been provoked by a (mostly Evangelical) movement that calls itself "creation science." Its key proposition is that the theory of evolution as taught by standard biology is not supported by the scientific evidence. "Creation science" is supposed to offer an alternative, supporting the biblical account of creation in the book of Genesis. The demand that this allegedly scientific theory be taught in public schools alongside standard biology has led to a flood of litigation. I will come to that in a moment. For now, I just want to make the point that here is another (not very sophisticated) attempt to do away with the boundary between religious and secular discourses by claiming the legitimating banner of "science" for a religious worldview.

Not surprisingly, for a long time the schools have been principal battlefields in boundary disputes between secular and religious discourses. This was an inevitable development as universal and compulsory education was established in every modern state, from the nineteenth century on – first in elementary schools, then extending to secondary schools as well. There are few human rights as close to most people's hearts as the right to raise one's children according to one's own values. This concern was directly touched when the state compelled parents to send their children to state-approved schools, often staffed by teachers indifferent or hostile to parents' religions. In many cases the dispute over the place of religion in school curricula had an ethnic component, where religious divisions corresponded to ethnic ones. That was the case in the last fifty years of the Habsburg monarchy, a case that was eerily replicated in the religio-ethnic conflicts which, another half-century on, led to the dismantling of the Yugoslav state. In countries where the state promulgated an ideological secularism, the conflict over schools became particularly sharp, with France during the Third Republic being an important case in point, particularly after the separation of church and state in 1905. Down to the village level, the conflict between schoolteacher and priest often became a central political reality. Modern education, especially in the natural sciences and mathematics, necessarily gives pride of place to a secular discourse, "as if God did not exist," provoking religious institutions and ordinary believers to resist the encroachment of this secularity on the relevance structure of religion and its place in public life.

At the time of writing, Israel provides a vivid illustration of such a conflict. There is a separate school system for Israeli Arabs, but the Jewish schools have been very much affected by the demographic expansion of the ultra-Orthodox or Haredi populations, who have much larger fertility rates as compared to secular or just moderately observant Israelis. It is estimated that about 20 % of Jewish children are now in Haredi schools. That percentage is bound to grow. The curriculum in Haredi schools overwhelmingly focuses on the traditional study of Torah and Talmud. The graduates of these schools are notoriously unemployed and unemployable in the highly modern economy of the country. The government has been pushing for a minimal curriculum of non-religious subjects in Haredi schools, including natural sciences and mathematics as well as English language instruction. This effort has met with fierce resistance from the Haredi community, which is a minority of the Jewish population but has great influence due to its sway over important political parties and the radical form of proportional representation in the Israeli election system. The growth of a chronically uneducated (in modern terms) and therefore unemployed segment of the population not only puts an increasing burden on the quite generous Israeli welfare state but in the not-so-long run endangers the future of the hitherto successful Israeli economy. Arguably, this is developing into an existential question for the future of the state.

Every modern society depends on a technological and organizational infrastructure that is necessarily based on a secular discourse. This discourse thus has a privileged position in public life, even if it is limited (as in the United States) by rigorous legal protections of religious freedom. Americans are notoriously addicted to litigation, thus the courts have been full of cases involving the boundaries of religious and secular relevance structures. As is to be expected, many of them are concerned with issues in public schools. The aforementioned issue of creationism has been an important instance. In parts of the country where Evangelicals are strong, there has been a campaign to have so-called "creation science" taught in public schools alongside standard science courses. Courts are understandably reluctant to take positions on disputed areas of science, but here they were compelled to decide what was science and what was not. They decided that evolution was established scientific fact, while the idea that the earth was only some six thousand years old was not based on science but on religious belief; therefore, taxpayers should not pay for it in public schools. The conflict became more complex when the issue morphed from creationism to so-called "intelligent design," the proposition that the universe could not be understood unless it was understood as a product of intelligence (presumably, although this point was not emphasized, that of an intelligent designer or creator). I think this proposition is likely to be affirmed by any believer, at least in the monotheistic religions. However, the proponents of "intelligent design" were not content with making this argument; they insisted that the argument was a scientific one, therefore eligible as a science curriculum to be supported by the taxpayers. Again, the courts were faced with the need to define what is scientific fact; again, they decided (correctly, I think) that "intelligent design" was not a scientific theory but an expression of religious faith. Individuals and churches are free to proclaim this faith from pulpits, on street corners, and in schools they support, but not in science classes paid for by taxpayers.

There is another set of cases in which American courts, explicitly or implicitly, reaffirmed the privileged status of the secular discourse of science. In a recent case, there again appeared the issue of whether parents could be prosecuted for criminal neglect if, for religious reasons, they failed to provide timely medical care for a seriously ill child. This issue has often surfaced with Jehovah's Witnesses, who are theologically opposed to blood transfusions. There was one complicating factor in this particular case, because the defense argued that the parents were reasonable in waiting some time before calling for medical assistance; however, the parents were open in stating that their faith told them to pray for divine healing in lieu of any modern medical intervention. Whatever the outcome of this case, American courts have generally held that modern medicine is factual in a way that any religious belief is not. In another interesting case, a preacher was sued for ceremonially cursing an individual. This was not a criminal case but rather a civil case under tort law. The plaintiff lost the case, because the judge decided that a curse could not cause real damage. One can easily imagine how this case would have been decided in, say, Puritan New England. In any event, here again a court affirmed the privileged status of a scientifically based "naturalist" worldview over any "supernatural" scheme of interpretation. It should be noted that there was no prohibition by the court of curses being uttered by a preacher or, for that matter, by any religiously infuriated lay person; there was just the statement that the court had to decide the case on the basis of a secular discourse. One may add that this would be so even if the judge or one of the jurors personally believed in the efficacy of curses.

Shmuel Eisenstadt was correct in his thesis about multiple modernities. There could be modern societies in which the boundaries between religion and secularity could be drawn differently than is currently done in the United States or other Western democracies. Could Israel remain a modern society if the Haredi version of Jewish religious law came to be officially established? Perhaps, though some modifications of the Haredi ideology would be required; El Al Airlines could not be run on Halachah principles, and, if a Haredi-dominated educational system did not produce enough technologically competent Israelis, foreigners would have to be recruited to run the airline. The United States could still function as a modern society if, say, Texas allowed "creation science" to be taught in schools alongside modern scientific biology, though bioengineering firms might hesitate to hire graduates of the Texas educational system.

 In conclusion, I would like to reiterate the main points of the last two chapters. There is a pluralism of religious discourses in the minds of individuals and in society. There is also the centrally important pluralism between secular and religious discourses. Also, there is a pluralism of different versions of modernity, with different delineations of the co-existence of religion and secularity. Pluralism must be politically managed; the next chapter will take up that issue.

Further Reading

Bellah, Robert N. *Tokugawa Religion: The Cultural Roots of Modern Japan*. 2nd ed. New York: Free Press, 1985.

Cohen, Asher, and Bernard Susser. *Israel and the Politics of Jewish Identity: The Secular-Religious Impasse*. Baltimore: The Johns Hopkins University Press, 2000.

Eisenstadt, S.N. "Multiple Modernities." *Daedalus* 129, no. 1 (January 1, 2000): 1–29.

—. *Japanese Civilization: A Comparative View*. Chicago: University Of Chicago Press, 1996.

Jelen, Ted G., ed. *Sacred Markets, Sacred Canopies: Essays on Religious Markets and Religious Pluralism*. Lanham: Rowman & Littlefield, 2002.

Larson, Edward J. *Summer for the Gods: The Scopes Trial and America's Continuing Debate over Science and Religion*. New York: Basic Books, 2008.

Sachsenmaier, Dominic, Shmuel N. Eisenstadt, and Jens Riedel, eds. *Reflections on Multiple Modernities: European, Chinese and Other Interpretations*. Leiden: Brill, 2002.

Chapter 6: The Political Management of Pluralism

I have argued that a useful theory of religious pluralism must combine the individual and the political components of the phenomenon. Usually the two components are discussed separately. To return to a previous example, there are two questions troubling millions of people in the contemporary world. The first is, "How can I, a believing and practicing Muslim, also be a modern person?" The second is, "What could and should a modern Islamic society look like?" The two questions belong together. Answering one will help answer the other. It hardly needs emphasizing that finding answers to these particular questions is of urgent importance today. Religious traditions other than Islam also raise comparable questions, even if not necessarily with the same political urgency.

Religious pluralism produces two distinct political problems: how the state defines its own relation to religion, and how the state sets out to regulate the relations of different religions with each other. In practical terms, this leads to a search for what I propose to call formulas of peace. In other words, it becomes necessary to define formulas for a peaceful co-existence of different religious traditions and institutions within a society. This problem is not new. Religious pluralism has existed in previous periods of history, and quite different formulas of peace have been devised. These are interesting in themselves. Anyone concerned with the political problems of our own time will be concerned with the usefulness of the various formulas for dealing with the issue today.

There was religious pluralism in the late Roman Empire, which was in some ways similar to our own. In the New Testament, the account of the visit to Athens by the Apostle Paul provides a vivid picture. Paul himself describes the many altars he saw in the city. He could have had similar experiences in Alexandria, or Antioch, or even in Rome, though a few miles outside such metropolitan centers one could still visit much more religiously homogeneous places. There was a high degree of religious pluralism on the Silk Road that for centuries linked the Mediterranean world and China, where Christianity (in different versions) interacted with Manichaeism, Zoroastrianism, Buddhism, Confucian scholarship, and the remnants of Greek culture originally brought there by Alexander the Great. There was also religious pluralism for longer or shorter periods in Muslim Spain and Mughal India, as mentioned above. However, there are two important differences of these pluralisms from religious pluralism today.

One difference if the sheer geographical scope of the current phenomenon. Pentecostal and Mormon missionaries can be found almost anywhere in the world today. Much of Latin America, once solidly Catholic, now contains huge

Protestant communities. Christianity is exploding in China. Hare Krishnas dance and chant in front of medieval cathedrals in Europe. Tens of thousands of Europeans and Americans are engaged in meditational practices originating from southern and eastern Asia. If one wants to get away from the global pluralist dynamic, one will have to visit villages deep in the jungles of central Africa or Amazonia. Even there, one had better not bring along one's laptop. If one can find a way of connecting it with the Internet, the pluralist cacophony will reach one even in the depths of the primeval rainforest, if one has not already come across some of the aforementioned intrepid missionaries.

There is another important difference from previous pluralisms, and that is the powerful presence of the secular discourse, which I discussed in an earlier chapter. If a medical clinic has been set up in a remote corner of the rainforest, its definitions of reality will collide with those of the local witchdoctor, and the collision in the village square will be replicated in the minds of patients seeking help from either source.

Historically, an important formula of peace, particularly favored by those who held or aspired to political power, was peace through official indifference. It was certainly the formula employed by those in charge of the Roman Empire. That situation was succinctly captured in a statement by the historian Edward Gibbon: "The common people thought that all religions were equally true, the philosophers that all religions were equally false, the magistrates that all religions were equally useful" (or, as the case may be, equally useless). Thornton Wilder, in *The Ides of March*, his novel about Julius Caesar, described this attitude very well. Wilder's Caesar did not believe in the gods and thought that all of the ceremonies around the Vestal Virgins and the official augurs were nothing but superstition. However, once Caesar was in a position of power, he participated in all the ceremonies, thinking that they served to legitimate his power. In this connection, it is worthwhile to recall the attitude of Roman authorities toward Christians. The Roman magistrates who persecuted Christians could not have cared less about their beliefs, such as the idea that an obscure Jewish prophet was believed to be divine and to have risen from the dead. What bothered the authorities was that Christians refused to participate in the imperial cult, which was the most important ceremony signifying loyalty to the Empire. To avoid persecution, Christians were not required to recant any of their beliefs; they only had to show the receipt given to a person after participation in the ceremonies of the imperial cult. Christians risked their lives in avoiding these rituals, which they considered a blasphemous violation of their first commandment. I find it curious that a few millennia later, in a comparable case, another group of Christians reached the opposite conclusion. In the 1930s, under the military regime in Japan, participation in the Japanese imperial cult was a compulsory act of patriotic citizenship. The Kyodan, which was the federation of the small Protestant community in Japan, decided that Christians could in good conscience participate in this ritual, since (although it implied the divine status of the Emperor) it was not an expression of religious faith but only of political allegiance. The regime itself distinguished the official State Shinto (of which the imperial cult was the ritual core) from so-called sectarian Shinto, with its bundle of religious beliefs and practices. The American military government set up after World War II implicitly reaffirmed that distinction, prohibiting State Shinto but not interfering with what went on in the many temples of popular Shinto.

Roman magistrates were not alone in following a formula of peace based on indifference (if not contempt). Gibbon's above-quoted description could be applied directly to the classical Confucian attitude to religion. It can be plausibly argued that Confucianism, although based on certain quasi-religious presuppositions (such as the "mandate of heaven" that bestows legitimacy on a government), is a this-worldly system of ethics rather than a bundle of religious doctrines. The mandarins, the political elite of the Confucian political order, were very much concerned with *li*, the correct performance of official ceremonies, but tended to look down on the religion of the masses, including the allegedly superstitious beliefs and practices of Buddhism and Daoism, not to mention the numerous "kitchen gods" and local spirits of Chinese folk religion. I think that this Confucian heritage is surprisingly relevant to government policy toward religion in the People's Republic of China today. Invocations of Marxism and of Mao Zedong are useful *li* to celebrate the power of the Communist Party (if you will, its "mandate of heaven"). I doubt if many in the Party elite today believe in any of the Marxist or Maoist doctrines. Their attitude to religion impresses me as essentially Confucian. Religion can be a factor of stability; Christianity may meet this criterion, even more so if it promotes the "Protestant ethic" deemed to be useful for modern economic development, a Party goal. So, maybe, Christianity could be a useful thing, especially if its adherents do not push for human rights and democracy (as they did, *exemplum horribile*, in Taiwan and South Korea). By contrast, Buddhism is not useful in Tibet, and neither is Islam among the Uigurs; in both regions, these religions supposedly encourage "splittism." For some years now the Chinese regime has relentlessly repressed the Falun Gong cult. I don't think that the regime was motivated by concerns for public health, though it is probably right that the alleged health benefits of the cult's meditation techniques are highly questionable. What drove the regime crazy was that Falun Gong could bring some ten thousand followers to Beijing for a conference, without the authorities being aware of it. If Communists know one thing, it is the revolutionary potential of mass meetings.

In the case of Christianity, Pontius Pilate, the Roman governor of Judea, was very much an educated member of his class; when Jesus, having been taken to him for judgment, said that he had come to witness to the truth, Pilate contemptuously replied, "What is truth?" He could not care less about what in his view were the Jewish superstitions that were at issue in this case. He certainly cared about the stability of Roman rule in this province. When Christianity became the state religion in one country after another, in the centuries following its official recognition by the Emperor Constantine, the attitude of rulers was not too different from that of Pontius Pilate.

Constantine was a convert to Christianity, possibly for superstitious reasons of his own – a vision of the Cross with the promise before an important battle that "in this sign you will win." However, I don't think it was theological considerations that made him convoke the Council of Nicea, which defined the contours of Christian orthodoxy. Constantine had the very Roman conviction that religious squabbles were potentially destabilizing. Centuries later, King Frederick the Great of Prussia expressed the same attitude when he said (also in a contemptuous tone), "Let everyone be redeemed according to his own fashion." Catholics' fashion in matters of redemption was definitely suspect in Frederick's decidedly Protestant state, but so were intra-Protestant disputes. There was the potentially destabilizing fact that most Prussian subjects were Lutherans, while the ruling dynasty was Reformed/Calvinist. Supposedly this was not good, so the government decreed that the two Protestant denominations should be merged into one church, the so-called Prusssian Union, which had a synthetic theology and a liturgy to go with it. Its Protestantism was defined as both Lutheran and Reformed. It may be noted here that some of the early Lutheran immigrants to America were dissidents who rejected the Prussian merger, holding on to what they thought was unadulterated (*echt*) Lutheranism.

Religion has been politically instrumentalized many times since then. American politicians are served today by election technicians who, whatever their own convictions, can have clients with contradictory views. Thus politicians of either party running in states with strong Evangelical constituencies will obviously want to attract voters from this population. Election technicians can advise them what to say, when, and to whom; an atheist can be just as effective in this as a believing Evangelical, perhaps even more so, because a believer may be reluctant to instrumentalize their faith to this degree. There are limits to this kind of cynicism. On the other hand, a highly secularized election advisor from San Francisco may have difficulty sounding like a fervent Southern Baptist in Arkansas. Some are faster learners than others, and I imagine that some politicians are more cynical than others.

India has produced an interesting and quite idiosyncratic formula of peace, which one might call peace through absorption. While Hinduism is a religion with many doctrines (including monotheism, pantheism, and atheism), though not what one could call an orthodoxy or binding doctrine, as well as an emporium of rituals, it has for many centuries contained an internal pluralism. This pluralism is represented by schools of devotion (*bhakti*) that almost resemble different denominations, for example the devotees of Vishnu, Shiva, and yet other gods. It has been argued that what really holds the tradition together is the system of caste, a uniquely Indian institution (though it has extended to a few other countries, notably Indonesia, with Bali the most Hinduized island in the archipelago). Most interesting is the fact that other religious communities in India have created their own castes, including the hierarchy from Brahmins on top to what used to be referred to as Untouchables (now called Dalits) at the bottom. Thus there are Jain castes, Sikh castes, and, despite the basic egalitarianism of Christianity and Islam, Christian castes and Muslim castes. The states of Kerala and Goa have the highest percentage of Christians, and elaborate Christian caste systems, which are now having to cope (just like Hinduism proper) with a Dalit movement for equal rights. The sense of caste goes very deep, even including bodily reactions. I was once told the following story by a Protestant missionary. A high-caste Hindu had been converted to Christianity; I think he joined the Church of South India, which had resulted from a merger of Anglicans with other Protestant groups. The missionary who told me the story had no doubts about the genuineness of the conversion. The time came for the first communion of the new convert. He noticed with apprehension that several Dalits were kneeling close to him, about to receive the sacrament. In his mind he was about to have a meal with ritually impure people – the ultimate caste taboo. That perception was not only in his mind; it involved his body. He knew that it was his Christian duty to take communion with them. He forced himself to do so, but as soon as the host was in his mouth, he had to rush out and vomit. Thus one could define a Hindu not by what he believes, but by what makes him vomit.

Sooner or later, it seems, everyone in India becomes a caste; just as in the United States, everyone, even Judaism, produces denominations. I am not an expert on Indian caste today. It has proven to be a very resilient institution, though in much of the country (especially in urban areas) it is less powerful than it used to be. Hindu nationalists have proposed that Hinduism is not a religion but a civilization, which they call *hindutva* (Hinduness). They want Muslims, who make up about ten percent of the population of India, to accept this. Few do. I doubt if the ideology of *hindutva* will ultimately work as a plausible contemporary formula of peace even within India. It is difficult to imagine that caste could serve as such anywhere else. Historically, however, it is certainly a unique and interesting attempt.

While caste as a formula of peace to manage religious pluralism will have little traction outside India and has less than uniform consensus even among Hindus there, one of the most urgent questions in the contemporary world is how religious pluralism can or should be managed in a society that defines itself as Islamic. Of course there are large differences of opinion about this in most if not all Muslim-majority countries, especially those (which actually is most of them) that aspire to be Islamic as well as modern, albeit within certain limits. This issue, for understandable reasons, is commonly discussed today in terms of the question of whether Islam is compatible with democracy. Of course this is an important question, but there is the more basic question of the relation of Islam with modernity. After all, there have long been modern societies that were or are not democratic. The former Soviet republics in Central Asia, and their independent successor states, offer interesting examples. In other words, before we can ask what an Islamic democracy could or should look like, we must ask about the character of an Islamic modernity. In line with the discussions in the earlier chapters of this book, this also involves the question of the place of the secular discourse in an Islamic society. Obviously, there must be such a place in some areas of society – notably, where the society utilizes institutions based on modern technology, from airlines to hospitals, but also where the society interacts successfully with a global economy that requires all actors to follow a specifically modern rationality. The history of Islam shows that these questions cannot be answered simply.

There are two distinct sub-questions here: how to manage the co-existence of Islamic and secular discourses, and how to manage the co-existence of different religious traditions within a Muslim state. Islamic law, the *sharia*, has always been all-embracing, ordering the structure of the state and the details of everyday life. There are different schools of Islamic law, some more flexible than others on these issues. Yet it is important to keep in mind that Islam, in addition to affirming a universal, transnational Muslim community, the *umma*, also established overtly Muslim states, the rulers of which often fought wars with each other and whose actions necessarily had to conform to the harsh demands of *raison d'etat*. Presumably there was little if any tension between the requirements of the faith and of the state when Muhammad himself established the very first Muslim state in Medina. As soon as Islam dominated a geographically expansive empire, beginning with the Ummayad caliphate, which was ruled from Damascus, many state actions could adequately be explained in terms of principles commonly called Macchiavellian. Needless to say, in this Islam differs little from Christianity, which from early on posited a universal Christian church but also became the official creed of states that often acted in ways hard to reconcile with the teachings of Jesus. As to managing religious pluralism in such states, for a very long time tolerance of other faiths (including diverse interpretations of the Christian faith) was not a salient characteristic of these states.

Historically, as defined in *sharia* law and mentioned above, the world is divided into two realms – the House of Islam (*Dar al-Islam*) and the House of War (*Dar al-harb*). In principle, then, a state of warfare exists between the two, although for various practical reasons there may be periods of truce or armistice, *hudna*, between them. There can be no question that a vast Muslim world was established by means of armed conquest. Its memory continues to animate perspectives and actions in the Muslim world to this day. Just a few years after Muhammad's death, Muslim armies swept out of Arabia, defeated the Byzantine and Persian empires that between them had dominated the Middle East, and set up Muslim states from North Africa and Spain to the borders of India. It is part of political etiquette in some circles today to downplay this martial history. In the immediate wake of the events of September 11, 2001, President George W. Bush (no doubt with laudable intentions) said that the United States was not at war with Islam but with terrorists advocating a distorted version of Islam. He also said that "Islam means peace." It does not. Peace in Arabic is *"salaam."* Every time a Muslim greets someone, they wish peace upon that person, *"Salaam aleikum."* It is a beautiful custom, but it does not define Islam. The word for Islam derives from the Arabic *aslama*, "to submit." This history creates great difficulties for a secular discourse and for religious pluralism within the House of Islam.

As in the case of other religious traditions, Islam has had to deal with two related but distinct issues – how to cope with religious pluralism in a Muslim society, and how to deal with the pluralism of religious (in this case Islamic) and secular discourses. As far as the first issue is concerned, early in its history Islam devised its own formula of peace. It could be described as peace by subordination. The state is an Islamic entity, but non-Muslim religious communities are tolerated and protected in a subordinate status. This formula goes back to the Quran. It is based on the understanding of Muhammad as being the culmination of a series of preceding prophets, which include Abraham, Moses, and Jesus. The followers of these earlier prophets are designated as People of the Book. Originally, in the state of Medina that was ruled by the Prophet in person, this designation referred to Jews and Christians. Later, as the Muslim world expanded, Zoroastrians, Hindus, and even Buddhists were included under this category. Such non-Muslim subjects were given the status of *dhimmi* – barred from rights and obligations reserved for Muslims, but, in return for a special tax, being guaranteed the right to worship and jurisdiction over their internal affairs, in matters such as marriage and inheritance. Significantly, there was no discrimination between Muslims and non-Muslims in matters of property rights and contract law, thus giving wide scope to economic activity by non-Muslims. Some schools of Islamic law accord *dhimmi* status to all non-Muslims who subject themselves to the authority of a Muslim state.

In today's perspective, especially in terms of our current notions of human and civil rights, the *dhimmi* status is highly discriminatory and degrading, a form of second-class citizenship not consonant with the rule of law and the values of democracy. I imagine that it was experienced in this way by many *dhimmis* in the past, and there were periods when even these lesser rights were violated by more intolerant Muslim regimes. Nevertheless, it is noteworthy that for many non-Muslims this formula of peace allowed them to prosper and live in considerable comfort, especially as compared with their condition under repressive Christian governments. I have already mentioned the pluralism of the Ottoman Empire, in which many Jews found refuge after their expulsion from Spain. I should also mention the fate of the so-called Oriental or non-Chalcedonian Christians (specifically Monophysites and Nestorians, who rejected the Christological doctrines promulgated by the early church councils), who were severely repressed in the Orthodox Byzantine Empire. Many of them fled to Muslim states, where they were protected as People of the Book. There was a period of so-called *conviviencia* – peaceful co-existence and interaction between Muslims, Christians and Jews – under the Caliphate of Cordoba. There were similar episodes in Mughal India. This formula of peace continued quite effectively in the so-called *millet* system of the Ottomans; each *millet* was granted officially recognized jurisdiction over Jews and different varieties of Christians. The concept of "Ottoman civility" has been applied by some historians to this phenomenon; needless to say, it was occasionally suspended in eruptions of persecution, but it was quite real over extended periods of time. After the collapse of the Ottoman Empire it was, perhaps ironically, taken over by British and French colonial regimes in the Arab world, and more recently by the State of Israel. It should be noted that, under this formula, a kind of religious freedom is accorded to communities, not to individuals.

There is no comparable traditional Muslim formula for what I would call "the other pluralism" – that between Islamic and modern discourses. *Sharia* is all-embracing, providing both an order for the state and for the most intimate minutiae of personal life. Thus it is more difficult to carve out an exempt area for this or that secular discourse. As far as modern technology and (to a lesser degree) modern economics are concerned, this is relatively manageable, though there is an issue with Islamic notions about usury inhibiting participation in the global banking system. Not even the most fundamentalist Salafi expects Islamic rulings, *fatwas,* to decide how to fly a jet airliner or to perform brain surgery.. Earlier I mentioned the experiment by which King Ibn Saud "proved" that the telephone is not an instrument of the devil. There is no comparable experiment to enable a secular discourse being allowed to govern areas of political and social life. That is the issue around which debates are now revolving.

Turkey has been at the forefront of these debates, especially since an Islamist party, the AKP (Adalet ve Kalkınma Partisi, or Justice and Development Party), was elected to power. It is not clear at this moment where this experiment of an Islamic democracy is going, but an early statement of the AKP agenda is still interesting: "We don't want a *sharia* state; we want to live as good Muslims in a secular republic." At the time of writing, and in a different context, the debate over the Egyptian constitution clearly shows two different directions in which an Islamist agenda could go. One formulation says that legislation should be based on "Islamic rulings" – that is, specific *fatwas* by Islamic courts. The other formulation says that legislation should be based on "Islamic principles." Obviously there is a large difference between the two formulations. Christian parallels to these formulations are easy to find in recent history. The Franco regime, established as the outcome of the Spanish Civil War (1936 – 1939), was the last attempt to set up an explicitly Christian (in this case, "integrally Catholic") state. By contrast, the movement of Christian democracy, mostly Catholic in inspiration, which played an important role in the politics of Western Europe after World War II, had a very different, much looser understanding of the relation of Christianity to the secular democratic state. The debates about this issue among Muslims today are of very great importance for the future of a large segment of the world and the latter's relations with globalized society. Many factors, most of them non-theological, will influence the outcome. I would rather timidly venture a prediction: It is unlikely that many Muslim-majority countries will adopt a strict separation of mosque and state along the lines of the American or French constitutions. More likely, the outcome will be somewhere between the two above-mentioned alternatives, with the constitution and subsequent legislation being based on either "Islamic rulings" or "Islamic principles." People committed to the First Amendment to the US Constitution or the *laïcité* at the heart of French republicanism will have to decide whether they find one or both Islamist projects acceptable.

As has been pointed out many times, there is an interesting similarity between Islamic and Jewish religious law. Both traditions define themselves in terms of such law. It is noteworthy that in Arabic the same word, *din,* which literally means "law", also refers to a religious tradition. Thus an Arabic speaker who wants to ask about someone's religion, will ask "what is your *din?*" A Protestant will have great difficulty answering this question, as might a Catholic;

Roman canon law, for instance, doesn't regulate what is done in the kitchen. An observant Jew will have no such difficulty. *Halacha*, like *sharia*, is all-embracing – ranging from the counsels of state to the activities in kitchen or bedroom. However, there is an important difference. In the roughly two millennia between the destruction of the last Jewish state by the Romans (70 CE) and the establishment of the State of Israel (1948), there was no Jewish government that could enforce any element of *halacha*. There is of course a very different situation in Israel today, with its curious continuation of the Ottoman *millet* system. Whatever arrangement between Jewish religion and secular democracy the Israelis end up with, it is unlikely to be emulated in any other country. All the same, as one looks at different formulas of peace, the Israeli debates can be quite instructive.

In modern Western history there have been two enormously important formulas of peace relevant to religious pluralism: that of the Imperial Diet of Augsburg and of the Peace of Westphalia, and that of the more recent separation of state and church. The latter has strongly influenced the understanding of religious freedom in international human rights discourse. The Diet of Augsburg was convened by the Emperor Charles V in 1555 in order to arrive at some sort of peace between Catholics and Protestants. The Emperor, who was a very conservative Catholic, would have liked nothing better than to completely extirpate the nascent Protestant movement. He was held back from this pious action by the looming danger of the Ottoman Turkish invasion, which required a reasonably united Christian response, supported by both Catholic and Protestant princes. The Lutherans submitted their own theological position (ever since known as the Augsburg Confession), which the Emperor respectfully read, though of course without agreeing with it. The formula was very clear and very influential: "*Cuius regio, eius religio*" ("Whose the rule, his the religion"). This means that each prince had the right to decide which faith, Catholic or Protestant, would prevail in his territory; those of his subjects who disagreed were free to emigrate. This was not exactly freedom of religion as we now understand it, but it was certainly an improvement over being massacred or forcibly converted. The formula was not immediately put into practice, but in 1648 it was reiterated and became the basis of the Peace of Westphalia, a series of international treaties (signed in Münster and Osnabrück) that established the modern concept of sovereign states and ended the horrible bloodshed of the Thirty Years' War. This time around, this formula of peace was realized to a high degree in the lands belonging to the Holy Roman Empire. It now included not only Catholics and Lutherans but also Calvinists, who had come to power in the newly independent Netherlands and several Swiss cantons.

This was of course a territorial formula of peace, assuming that the population of each territory would either be religiously homogenous to begin with or would come to be so as a result of the formula. The increasing religious plural-ism in an increasing number of Western countries makes this formula ever more difficult to realize in practice, in Europe or elsewhere. Wherever it has been tried, it has led to the high, often horrendous human costs of religio-ethnic "cleans-ing." This occurred with the forced exchanges of populations between Greece and Turkey in the early 1920s, the massacres and flows of refugees following the partition of India in 1947, and more recently in the wars following the disin-tegration of Yugoslavia. Given this record, it is not surprising that this formula of peace has not been recommended very often. It has been talked about, with little enthusiasm on either side, in discussions of a possible settlement of the Israeli-Palestinian conflict.

The other important Western formula of peace has been the concept of the separation of church and state, developed by the thinkers of the Enlightenment and realized in the wake of the American and French revolutions. The concept has been successfully applied to both of the two pluralisms that I proposed above – the pluralism of diverse religious traditions and institutions, and the pluralism of secular and religious discourses. This double application has been classically formulated in the two clauses of the First Amendment to the US Constitution – one proscribing an establishment of religion, the other guar-anteeing the free exercise of religion. There is some tension between the two clauses, creating occasions of endless litigation to this day. The goal here, which has been largely achieved, is to carve out a niche in law and in the work-ings of the state in which a strictly secular discourse is the only one permitted, but which also co-exists with a great variety of religious discourses. Thus, for ex-ample, a federal judge who is a believing and practicing Christian, with strongly negative views on same-sex marriage, should render a decision in a case involv-ing this matter only on the basis of secular law, with no reference to any religious beliefs or values.

In one way or another, all Western democracies operate under a separation of church and state, albeit in different versions. The American version is very dis-tinctive. The legal separation is very strict, in some ways stricter than the French version, which is often cited in opposition. Thus, for example, it would be uncon-stitutional in the US for tax funds to be used to pay for the salaries of teachers in religious schools, which is routinely done in France and incidentally also in Tur-key, where secularism was instituted on the French model by Kemal Ataturk. At the same time, American politics hosts a cacophony of religious discourses, which would be quite unthinkable in most of Europe today. During the time when Tony Blair was prime minister of the United Kingdom, one of his spokes-men was asked why Blair, who was known to be a very religious person, never spoke about religion in public. The spokesman gave a marvelous reply: "We don't do God here!" This pronouncement describes the behavior of most politicians in Western and Central Europe today.

A radical separation of state and church was instituted in France in 1905, after the republican side won over the conservative side in the conflict centered on the Dreyfus affair. The ideal of *laïcité* (literally "lay-ness") expresses this understanding of the republic very clearly. For practical reasons, the state will enter into negotiations with religious bodies, for example in matters of education. Indeed, where such bodies do not exist, the state will help their coming to be so that it will have someone to negotiate with; it has done this in the past with Jews, and more recently with Muslims. However, the state itself is swept clean of all religious symbols of any sort. I think it is not unfair to describe the original attitude behind this as a kind of disease control; religion is potentially dangerous, and while it is not practical and perhaps not morally acceptable to suppress it, it must be quarantined in separate religious institutions so as not to "infect" the rest of society. While the Enlightened philosophy that gave birth to this arrangement was quite hostile to religion, the consequences have actually benefited religious minorities, including Protestants, Jews, and Muslims, by protecting them from the potential danger posed by the Catholic majority, which is hardly a real danger today, but certainly was that before 1905.

As mentioned in a previous chapter, Britain is a very interesting example of the separation of church and state, where this separation is a social reality that is still denied in the official definition of the state. Britain is a highly secularized society, as much so as any other in Western Europe, yet the Church of England is still established by the state. Its bishops sit in the House of Lords, and the monarch is still its official head. Yet Elizabeth II has recently re-interpreted this title in a public statement. One of her titles is still "Defender of the Faith," and while the Queen reaffirmed her belief in the establishment of the Church of England, she added that she now considered herself to be "the defender of all the faiths represented in the United Kingdom." This grammatical change from "faith" to "faiths" signals a solemn endorsement of religious pluralism. There have been favorable responses to such a redefinition of the Anglican establishment by Catholic, Jewish, and Muslim commentators. The former Archbishop of Canterbury has repeatedly affirmed the acceptance of Islam as a legitimate member of the British religious landscape. On another issue, his current successor has made a very interesting statement, saying that, while he holds to the conservative Christian rejection of homosexuality, he will not oppose the legalization of same-sex marriage as proposed by the Cameron government. The state can define marriage any way it wants, but the church will not recognize the equivalence of the state's definition with the one it solemnizes in a Christian wedding. In other words, the Church of England has come to terms with what I have called "the two pluralisms."

Grace Davie, the distinguished British sociologist of religion, has advanced the following proposition: A strong established church is bad, both for the state and for religion, as it tends to use state power to enforce religious conformity, thus undermining political stability and the credibility of the faith. This is what the Anglican establishment did in the past. However, there can be good consequences to a weak establishment, which is good for the state because it enhances political stability and good for religion because it is no longer tainted by its association with worldly, often unjust power. The Church of England today would seem to support Davie's position.

There are yet other European versions of the separation of church and state, for example in Germany, where there has been a steady expansion of the number of churches granted the status and privileges of "corporations of public law," a designation originally limited to Protestants and Catholics but which now includes any sizable religious community that does not engage in blatantly illegal activities. What all versions of church-state separation in Western democracies have in common is a state which is religiously neutral (*de jure* or *de facto*) and which operates within a decidedly secular discourse ("as if God did not exist").

Most Catholics and Protestants in Europe and the United States have by now given up any project of a strong establishment of any particular religion, while respecting the right of religious citizens and communities to enter the democratic process and push for policies consonant with their values. As a result, there now are many examples of what a Christian modernity may look like.

At the present time, the outlier to this Western pattern is Russia. The Orthodox faith survived decades of Soviet totalitarianism, during which murderous persecution alternated with reluctant toleration, periodically interrupted by selective repression and campaigns to promote "scientific atheism." The post-Communist Russian state, bereft of other legitimating ideologies, has increasingly relied on nationalism for this purpose. As in earlier periods of history, Russian nationalism holds the Orthodox Church in a close embrace. The traditional term for this close relation between church and state has been *sinfonia* – church and state, as it were, singing from the same page of the hymn book. So far this "symphony" has stopped short of formal establishment, but under the Putin government the Russian Orthodox Church has been accorded a privileged place in society, while possible religious rivals (notably the Roman Catholic Church and various Protestant missionaries) have been harassed and discriminated against. The Orthodox Church has reciprocated by supporting the government both in domestic matters (such as repression of dissidents) and foreign policy (for example in the Middle East). The further course of this relationship will be determined by the political needs of the Russian government, which may push it in either direction. It should be noted that in recent decades there has been a revival of popular Orthodox piety, which has been far removed from the political actions of the Moscow Patriarchate. I can think of no better metaphor for this dualism than a recurring event in the Hermitage Museum in St. Petersburg. The Hermitage has a remarkable collection of publically exhibited icons. To the surprise of visiting tourists, and the chagrin of the Museum administration, ordinary Russians come in from time to time in order to kiss the icons and kneel in prayer before them.

The purpose of this book is analytic. It is not my intention here to push my own religious or political views, or to make policy recommendations. However, the argument of this chapter points toward a policy-relevant conclusion. Under modern conditions, some version of church-state separation is most likely to support a stable and humane political order capable of managing what I have called "the two pluralisms." This conclusion can be arrived at on objective empirical grounds, without recourse to any theological or philosophical grounds – if you will, on strictly "Macchiavellian" grounds. A couple of years ago I made such an argument in a public lecture in China, attended among others by party officials, who (for whatever it's worth) expressed agreement. Depending on the audience, I would make the same argument again, wearing the surgical mask of antiseptic, "value-free" social science.

There are good empirical reasons to be in favor of religious freedom in the context of a religiously neutral state. However, it is important to emphasize that political utility is not the principal reason why most people who favor freedom of religion (myself definitely included) do so. A theological argument can also be made, as was done very cogently at the Second Vatican Council, and since then in the teachings and practice of the Roman Catholic Church. I think a similar argument can be made by other Christian, Jewish, and Muslim thinkers. There is also a philosophical argument, independent of religious presuppositions, with which agnostics or atheists could agree. It touches on the key perception of what it means to be human. Pascal described the human condition as standing at the midpoint between "the nothing and the infinite" (le neant et l'infini). This situation is shrouded in mystery. Human beings have wondered at this mystery throughout history. Religion has been the principal vehicle for this wonder: Why is there something rather than nothing? What does it all mean? Where do I come from? What may I hope for? How should I live? Who am I? Freedom to pursue this wonder is a fundamental human right. This freedom sets a limit to the power of the state; it is a fundamental right that predates and outweighs democracy or any particular form of government. It requires no instrumental justification. If, as is the case, religious freedom also turns out politically useful, this may be looked upon as a benefit to be grateful for.

Further Reading

An-Na'im, Abdullahi Ahmed. *Islam and the Secular State: Negotiating the Future of Shari'a*. Cambridge: Harvard University Press, 2008.

Beneke, Chris. *Beyond Toleration : The Religious Origins of American Pluralism*. New York: Oxford University Press, 2006.

Ferguson, John. *The Religions of the Roman Empire*. Ithaca: Cornell University Press, 1985.

Kuru, Ahmet T. *Secularism and State Policies toward Religion: The United States, France, and Turkey*. New York: Cambridge University Press, 2009.

Monsma, Stephen V., and J. Christopher Soper. *The Challenge of Pluralism: Church and State in Five Democracies*. Lanham: Rowman & Littlefield, 2009.

Norris, Pippa, and Ronald Inglehart. *Sacred and Secular: Religion and Politics Worldwide*. New York: Cambridge University Press, 2004.

Putnam, Robert D., and David E. Campbell. *American Grace: How Religion Divides and Unites Us*. Simon & Schuster, 2010.

van der Veer, Peter. *Religious Nationalism: Hindus and Muslims in India*. Berkeley: University of California Press, 1994.

Yang, Fenggang. *Religion in China: Survival and Revival under Communist Rule*. New York: Oxford University Press, 2011.

Response by Nancy T. Ammerman:
Modern Altars in Everyday Life

The question of religion's presence and role in a modern world has occupied sociologists from the beginning, none more brilliantly or influentially than Peter Berger (1969). With his masterful synthesis of the foundational theorists, he gave sociologists critical ways to think about religion. It was one of the very first books I read in the field, and its first four chapters remain on my syllabus every time I teach an introductory course. In the last three chapters of *The Sacred Canopy*, Berger then exercised his skill in reading the western theological and philosophical tradition alongside those sociological texts, formulating a theory of secularization that was enormously persuasive, in large measure (as he has pointed out) because it made perfect sense of the very intellectual world inhabited by most of the people who read his book (Berger 1999).

For thirty years, I have had the privilege of engaging Berger in conversations about these ideas – one might even say that he is part of my plausibility structure. His intellectual hospitality was instrumental both in supporting the "Congregations in Changing Communities Project" that I directed and in launching the conversations that became my book on *Everyday Religion* (Ammerman 2006) and later the "Spiritual Narratives in Everyday Life" project. Like Berger, I have arrived at a place where I am convinced that understanding the variation in relationships between states and religions is among the most theoretically and practically important puzzles to address in understanding modern religion. I will return to that at the end, but I turn first to the question of pluralism, the modern conundrum Berger addresses in this present book. The notion of a "sacred canopy" that would crack under the pressure of competing worldviews was among the first aspects of Berger's grand synthesis to fall, and the present book lays out his own re-thinking. My work on that problem has also attempted to tackle both the pluralism of everyday interaction and the pluralism of consciousness in very grounded empirical projects, each of which owes a debt to the sustaining conversation that has taken place at 10 Lenox Street.

1. Pluralism in American Communities

Thinking about the pluralism of everyday interaction took shape for me in questions about the transformation of the relationship between religion and geography. By the early 1990s, it was increasingly clear that American communities were being changed in ways that were challenging religious groups to respond.[1] Population movement from countryside to city and from city to suburb had already been a reality for most of the twentieth century, but most of that movement had taken place within a religious landscape still dominated by the cultural and organizational structures of Protestant and Catholic Christianity. The small town Methodist who moved to the city could find a new Methodist church to attend, and Methodist denominational officials could establish new congregations whenever their planning departments discerned the likely presence of a new cluster of prospects. Even if some of those Methodists strayed into Presbyterian or Baptist churches, the people in those denominational pews were unlikely to challenge the American Protestant view of the world that new residents had brought with them.

The post-1980s world was another matter. The American economy no longer supported stable working-class jobs. Decaying neighborhoods might be gentrified, but the new residents might be gays and lesbians. And the migrants into American cities were more likely to be from villages in Guatemala or India than from small towns in Alabama. The ecology of jobs, populations, and religious communities was being significantly reshuffled. The reality of pluralism was not just a cognitive challenge, but also a challenge to the organizational infrastructure that had largely constituted the context in which Americans had developed religious views of the world.

People in the US had, of course, always had a degree of practical religious pluralism at their fingertips, a situation that had always made the European model of a single religious canopy a poor fit for a sociology of American religion. As Stephen Warner wrote in a widely influential 1993 overview, pluralism has been constitutive of the religious ecology here (Warner 1993). No Westphalian compromise shaped the US political and religious landscape around territorial religious monopolies. Every religious group in the US had to come to terms with being one among many. The Puritans could banish their Baptists and Quakers and witches for only so long before the arrival of a jumble of Europe's religious diversity made pragmatic tolerance a necessity (Butler 1990).

My question, however, was not about that larger societal and cultural set of norms around getting along. Nor was it about the internal conflicts individuals may feel in situations that are religiously alien. Rather, I was interested in discovering how organizations rearranged themselves in this complicated dance of diversity. Without a central state apparatus to plan and constrain, how do re-

---

1 This section on religion and community life draws on the findings published in *Congregation and Community* (Ammerman 1997a).

ligious organizations designed with one group in mind respond to the presence of Others? The answer, to the chagrin of everyone who has hoped that congregations might be locations of social integration, is that very few existing congregations transform themselves into communities of diverse commensality and cultural integration (cf. Emerson and Kim 2003). Some slowly die as their founding constituents move away and pass from the scene. A few do find ways to integrate new and old populations, with new styles of worship and new forms of leadership. That was easiest, we found, when the cultural divide was less dramatic – between professionals who are straight and professionals who are gay, for instance. But most prominently, religious change happened because new groups of people simply founded new congregations. Where a new population brought an entirely new religious tradition (Pakistani Muslims or Japanese Buddhists, for instance), new religious communities would be expected; but new gatherings were also likely to happen when the new arrivals were Mexican Pentecostals in an African American neighborhood or economically struggling African American Baptists in an affluent white Protestant neighborhood. Whether because of outright discrimination or because of the desire for a safe and comfortable religious "home," people were clearly arranging themselves into distinct religious communities – organizational-level expressions of the constitutive pluralism of the US religious way.

There are many reasons to worry about this response to pluralism. Not only can it surround social difference with a layer of religious legitimation, it can also reinforce an echo chamber of social, cultural, and political opinion, insulating participants from the discomfort of dissenting views. There are also, however, reasons to be less pessimistic. There is very good evidence that such particularistic religious communities provide what Nancy Fraser (1990) calls a "subaltern counterpublic." African American churches are the prototypical "safe space" where an oppressed population has expressed sorrow and hope, organizing a "public" when no other public place was available (Lincoln and Mamiya 1990; Du Bois 1903 [2003]). Congregations have also allowed immigrant communities to transmit customs, language, and values across generations, as well as connecting new arrivals to critical social services.[2] They provide opportunities for women to assume leadership roles, and they indirectly provide models and experience for democratic participation – all in the context of a larger culture that may be unlikely to give minority groups and suppressed populations opportuni-

---

2 There is a large literature on the role of congregations in immigrant incorporation. See for example Ebaugh and Chafetz (1999), Foley and Hoge (2007), Ecklund (2005), Kurien (2007), and Mooney (2009).

ties to participate quite so fully. In any situation where otherness is less than fully welcomed, designated spaces, often religious ones, are needed to maintain a free and distinct sustaining conversation (Warner 1999).

What also became apparent in studying all of those relatively homogenous congregations was that most were not so isolated after all. Not surprisingly, they sought out opportunities to collaborate and commune with religiously like-minded others; but they were also very likely to be engaged in work that connected them to a wide variety of religious and secular others. My research in the late 1990s documented the dense and overlapping networks that constitute the mechanism by which communities provide services and enrichment in the US (Ammerman 2005a; 2005b). Nonprofit organizations, both religious and secular, may be the primary delivery vehicle, but they are sustained both by public funds and by the human and material resources that are often channeled through religious congregations. Mexican Pentecostals and Pakistani Muslims may worship separately on the weekend, but they may also work side-by-side in a soup kitchen or building a Habitat for Humanity house. This "street level ecumenism" is yet another way that pluralism finds everyday expression in the US. As Berger writes here, people "manage to live in the pluralistic situation by managing it pragmatically. They engage in a *convivencia* with the 'others' in their social environment, avoiding direct contradictions and striking bargains on the basis of live-and-let-live. These bargains may or may not involve cognitive compromises between worldviews and values" (p. 13). Even if they disagree on how to name God, they can agree that God wants them to help people in need.

Robert Putnam and David Campbell (2010) have written persuasively about how this network of overlapping connections works at the individual level to mitigate the potential divisiveness of cultural and religious diversity. They note that nearly all Americans have friendship networks that include religiously diverse others. We work or play with a friend who "happens to be" from another religious tradition; and the good feeling rubs off, leading us to judge all the members of that tradition more favorably. Even more powerfully, we all seem to have at least one relative whose beliefs would condemn them to eternal damnation if we followed our own creeds fully; but because we also take our cue from how people behave, we are unlikely to shun the kindly "Aunt Susan." I have described this impulse as "Golden Rule Christianity" (noting that there is also a Golden Rule Judaism and equivalents in other traditions, as well) (Ammerman 1997b). When we have asked people in multiple research projects to describe what is most essential to their faith, they are very likely to say that it is how people live their lives – do they live by the Golden Rule. Pluralism of religious creed can be tolerated so long as a basic ethical code of conduct remains in place. People who "happen to be" religiously different, even if their beliefs are anathema, can be friends and fellow citizens when they follow the Golden Rule.

Confronted by multiple religious traditions, then, modern people have neither cognitively suppressed religious views of the world nor entirely privatized their differences. As I was in the midst of that first study of congregations, I remember making an important theoretical turn in my own thinking. No longer was I looking for evidence that modern pluralism was eroding religious belief and practice. Rather, I was looking for the specific circumstances that supported or undermined religious practice in the midst of plural religious alternatives.

2. Social Structures for Pluralism

In the US, it was clear to me that part of the answer to that question can be found in the equal legal standing granted to multiple religious traditions. "American exceptionalism" to the secularization story arises in large measure from the relative absence of state interference in religious life. The specific circumstances that allowed pluralism and modernity to co-exist here started with the particular form of church-state separation that evolved (Hatch 1989). The resulting, relatively open religious field allowed for a high level of adaptability, the accommodation of a huge range of religious diversity, and a comparatively high level of religious participation. It has never seemed to me that this was a matter of sheer numbers of religious options, or of market-like competition among them.[3] While the question of monopoly and competition in religious "markets" has taken on at least as much contentious urgency as the question of secularization itself, I have preferred to stay mostly on the sidelines of that debate (Ammerman 1997c). My assessment is that most of the complicated statistical algorithms intended to prove or disprove the effects of more or less competition failed to add any particular wisdom beyond the observation that human beings, left unhindered by state regulation and given a culture of organizational voluntarism, are likely to organize social institutions in which religious ideas and practices can be celebrated in the company of others who wish to mark the rhythms of their lives together. Under some social and legal circumstances, that is, religious pluralism can be the very hallmark of a thoroughly modern society.

As the theoretical battles raged in the 1990s over macro-level metanarratives about the relationship between religion and modern society, I also began to won-

---

3 Among the major players in this debate were Finke and Stark (1988), Iannaconne (1991), Chaves (1992), and Olson (1999).

der, "Whose story is this? How is it that this account of the modern world gained so much currency?" My first answer to that question was one based on observations of the gender dynamics of the fight (Ammerman 1994). Whether one could be both religious and modern was not a question being raised mostly by women. It had also become clear that it was more a European question than an American one. And as Berger began to point out in the late 1990s, it was certainly not a question in the emerging Global South (Berger 1999). Rather, he noted, it seemed the particular preoccupation of a Western intellectual and cultural elite, a group whose personal life histories often encompassed the passage from faith to doubt that they then took for granted in the human condition.

As Talal Asad (1993) has observed, that same Western elite class (which also happened in its earliest days to be dominantly Protestant) sought to understand the spiritual expressions of the rest of the world through a lens that was defined by religions and states as they knew and needed them to be. Like good Protestants, they expected religion to take the form of personally held beliefs. As savvy rulers, they made sure that "religion" was organized into the sorts of delimited enterprises and hierarchical structures of authority that would make regulation sensible. Both in the West and beyond, religion became what we could manage with our bureaucracies and count on our surveys – degrees of agreement with a small core of supernatural beliefs, frequency of attendance at organized collective services, membership in an identified religious tradition. Nevermind what a specific tradition or society understands its spiritual sensibility to be; if these measures are in decline, then secularization is happening.

3. Pluralism of Consciousness

In some circles, Asad's critique nearly brought the study of "religion" to its knees. Happily, many of us have found ways forward. Berger's modest definition of religion in this book – "a belief that there is a reality beyond the reality of ordinary experience, and that this reality is of great significance for human life" (p. 17) – mirrors the moves I have made, as well. Following Bellah (2011) and Taylor (2007), among others, I have simply observed that when people act in the consciousness of "something beyond" themselves, it matters. And like Berger, I have become convinced that most human beings are quite capable of both this sort of sacred consciousness and a more mundane everyday mode of being in the world. Neither mode will inevitably extinguish the other.

In this present book, Berger does critical theoretical work with this insight. Drawing on Schutz's notion of multiple realities, he fundamentally alters the notion that a religious consciousness must be a total worldview. He reminds us that religious realities, like all others, come in three varieties: an inner core of taken-for-granted assumptions about the way the world works, a structure of cognitive and normative lenses that we consensually share with our culture, and a layer of preferences and lightly held opinions that are held "until further notice." Religious beliefs and practices may reside in any of these domains, but even more importantly, Berger follows Schutz in recognizing that none of this is organized into a neatly integrated whole. We are quite capable of participating in multiple (sometimes conflicting) realities, moving among multiple plausibility structures with more and less ease. To depend on scientific and engineering evidence when driving one's car does not make one "really" a secular person, just as saying a prayer before starting the journey does not mean that religious rules will govern one's driving. These sorts of either-or distinctions help us hardly at all in understanding the relationship between religion and modern society. Equally unhelpful is the presumption of a historical trajectory from utterly sacred to utterly secular. As Mary Douglas (1983) observed in the 1980s, earlier generations were surely not living in a world nearly so enchanted as we moderns like to believe, but neither are we moderns living in a world as disenchanted as Weber and most of sociology since imagined (Weber 1958). To observe mundane empirical explanations emerging in science or medicine, "as if God does not exist," tells us little about where or whether other parts of life may be infused with spiritual presence.

My own journey to discarding the sacred-secular binary took me by way of narrative theory and Margaret Somers (1994), rather than by way of Schutz and phenomenology. The journey started with a sustained intellectual conversation beginning in 2000 at Harvard's Hauser Center, exploring how we should understand religious presence in public life. There, in the very heart of a culture shaped by a presumably secular mastery of the modern world, a group of scholars struggled with the theoretical and practical consequences of the reality that faith was clearly not absent in most of the public policy dilemmas they faced. We worked together to arrive at the proposition that we had to see that social service work and policy debates are often both religious and secular at the same time. As Ziad Munson, one of the participants, later wrote about the pro-life activists he was observing, the funerals held for aborted fetuses are both religious and political at the same time (Munson 2006). They use religious symbols, rituals, and consciousness to express "something beyond" at the same time that they send a political message about how our common life ought to be arranged.

I came to think of these multiple layers of meaning as multiple narratives. Following Somers, I have conceptualized religious identity as an individual autobiographical narrative (what Somers labels "ontological") by which persons orient their actions in ways that are in continuity with who they have perceived themselves to be, but which (like any script) allows improvisation and revision. That individual story, of course, is always in dialogue with the many "public narratives" of the institutions that constitute our shared lives. Whether as a family or a corporation, a team or a congregation, we share a story about who *we* are; and that story, too, is constantly being revised and improvised. Finally, we live inside a few master stories, or metanarratives (like Schutz's world-taken-for-granted) with such hegemonic power that we often do not see their authorial hand. What I suggested in a 2003 essay is that religious identity is like all other identities, residing in just this sort of multi-layered narrative (Ammerman 2003). Out of early socialization and deep existential experiences, an autobiographical narrative that may include any of a wide range of spiritual orientations emerges. Out of a more or less pro-secular hegemonic narrative may emerge an equally strong set of expectations about what sorts of spiritual presence and action one might expect. But both those internal narratives and the metanarratives are constantly staged in particular institutionalized social settings with their own expectations about the kinds of stories that can be told there. All three layers are always present, each can shape the others, and none is by definition beyond the reach of enchantment.

With that conviction about how religion might appear in modern contexts, I have spent much of the last decade fostering conversations about "lived religion" (McGuire 2008; Hall 1997) and engaged in research exploring the stories people tell about their everyday lives. The result of that work is a growing body of evidence about the ways modern people manage to be both religious and secular at the same time. In my own work, one result was an expansive definition of spirituality that includes divine actors, miracles, and mysteries, as well as "extra-theistic" invocations of awe, meaning seeking, ethical grounding, and the like (Ammerman 2013b). From the everyday stories of a wide array of Americans came episodes in which a reality beyond the ordinary appeared in many forms and places. Recognizing both this wide range of forms and the breadth of religion's presence in everyday life, then, allowed significant rethinking of possible approaches to the question of a pluralism of consciousness. As I wrote in the conclusion of *Sacred Stories, Spiritual Tribes:*

> Having asked a wide range of Americans to tell us about their everyday lives, the stories we have called spiritual narratives are distinct from the stories we have identified as mundane and ordinary. There is in these stories a consciousness of transcendence, a recognition of a sacred dimension that goes beyond the ordinary. It need not be embodied in a deity, although it very often is. It need not be systematized into a set of doctrines, although centuries of work by legions of theologians have provided ample resources. It need not be organized into legally-recognized institutions, although the modern world has tended to try. It

need not even have a name, although some forms of commonly used language seem inevitable in each society and time. When sociologists study religion, it is this sacred consciousness that is at the heart of our enterprise (Ammerman 2013a, 293).

Berger is surely right to emphasize in this book the way institutions form consciousness and to remind us that modern institutions are often fragile. What my own research suggests, however, is that conversations are the basic building blocks of a religious consciousness, and those conversations can transcend institutional boundaries, allowing religious realities out of their strictly religious institutional boxes. As Berger and Luckmann (1967: 152) put it, "The most important vehicle of reality maintenance is conversation." Religious consciousness is produced in conversation, carried by actors from one place to another, and re-deployed and re-worked in each new telling.

To emphasize this micro-level of religious culture production is not to join the privatization theorists, however. Nor is it to reduce religion to an organizing principle of individual consciousness (a "meaning system"). What I have found were, yes, individual people narrating the actions of their everyday lives, with some of those individuals more likely to weave a layer of spirituality into the fabric than others. At one level, this is individual private religious consciousness. Yet what I am describing is a religious consciousness that is socially produced and maintained, dependent on organized religious traditions, but not exclusively so. Sacred consciousness is neither confined to individual minds nor to self-contained religious institutions, but it is still social.

How and where spirituality entered the stories we heard in our research was shaped by the shared language and symbols people had learned in families and congregations, and it was sometimes constrained and sometimes encouraged by the particular social settings in question. There is evidence of the modern "differentiation" of social functions in what we heard, but it is by no means a complete segregation. Sacred consciousness was part of the story more often when the story was about family and home, for instance, than when it was about working as a business person. Working as an artist or scientist, however, was often interwoven with a spiritual sensibility, and anyone who had a religiously likeminded friend at work had a partner in at least occasionally seeing spiritual dimensions in mundane activities. In the world of health, most people recounted their efforts to eat right and stay healthy as utterly guided by secular science and education. Their response to serious illness and death, on the other hand, was often heavily laden with prayer and spiritual presence. The multiple layers of reality and multiple narratives are perhaps nowhere better seen than in the person who prays for God to guide the doctor's hand.

As Berger points out in this book, the presence of multiple realities, each perhaps primarily institutionalized in a particular sector of society, creates the possibility for conflict and doubt. There can be boundary disputes when a way of framing a situation is deemed inappropriate for the context. There can be doubts when sacred consciousness is crowded out by secular expertise. As the neo-institutionalists have argued, there are dominant logics at work in each organizational "field" (Friedland and Alford 1991). What has become increasingly clear in other studies of organizations, however, is that these logics are never airtight. Decades ago feminists began arguing that "the personal is political" and that inflexible boundaries between home and work were not good for people. They were pointing to the ways institutional boundaries were and should be more permeable than theorists (and some managers) have assumed them to be. Indeed there are sometimes conflicts – between a caring and relational consciousness and an efficiency and impersonality consciousness, for instance, as well as between a sacred consciousness and the expectations of "secular" institutions. The "cultural capital" (as Bourdieu [1991] would describe it) from one field might or might not be permitted and useful in another.

Berger describes the presence of multiple secular and sacred realities as "code switching." That is certainly apt, but I suspect it may still draw too clear a distinction between codes and the fields they belong to. Sometimes people are aware of moving back and forth, but just as often they seem to occupy a single location that is both secular and sacred at the same time. It is not that our intrinsic foundational reality is secular, while our extrinsic world of choice can be religious if we choose. Rather, I am convinced that the mix of sacred and secular is more like "Spanglish" than like being bilingual. Words from both languages appear in the same sentence, sometimes modified in ways not native to either language. A person eats a kosher vegetarian diet both to express religious devotion and to stay healthy. A scientist reads his journals with a prayerful attitude that opens his mind to the solution he has been puzzling over.

In neither of these cases is this a matter of utterly individual invention and choice, although it is that. These are modern actors, after all. They have developed their ways of seeing and acting in the modern world, however, through socially constructed and institutionalized arenas of conversation. One of the most striking results of listening to people talk about their everyday lives was discovering the degree to which participation in organized religion matters for maintaining a religious consciousness. These were not people chosen because they were especially pious or especially intentional about spiritual seeking. Rather, our sample included the full range from utterly unaffiliated and nonobservant to very actively and traditionally religious. They included Catholics, Protestants of all stripes, Jews, Mormons, pagans, and non-affiliates. They included men and women, young and old, African American and Euro-American (and a few Hispanics and Asians), highly educated and less so, well-off and less so. Those demographic differences, however, explained very little about whether they actively inhabited a spiritual consciousness. Rather, it was people who attend services more frequently – no matter which tradition they are in – who are most likely to carry a spiritual view of the world beyond the four walls of whatever place in which they worship.

4. The Social Organization of Modern Religious Consciousness[4]

The study of religion in the modern world, then, cannot afford to ignore congregations and other organized spiritual groups as sites of religious culture production (*contra* Bender et al. 2012). When people do not have regular sites of interaction where spiritual discourse is a primary lingua franca, they are simply less likely to adopt elements of spirituality in their accounts of who they are and what they do with themselves. If they do not learn the language, it does not shape their way of being in the world. They can neither speak of – nor perhaps even see – a layer of spiritual reality alongside the mundane, everyday world. Conversely, the more deeply embedded people are in organized sites of spiritually infused conversation, the more likely they are to carry strands of that conversation with them. Within the bounds of a religious community, people develop a way of talking about life that carries within it expectations about the presence of divine actors and the realities of mysteries beyond human comprehension and the normative goodness of living by the Golden Rule. As people chat over a potluck dinner or pray during a meeting of a women's group, the everyday stories they tell are likely to foreground spiritual interpretations. They come to think of sacred and secular as intertwined. What happens in these religious gatherings is not just a matter of otherworldly ritual and doctrinal teaching. What happens is the creation of a particular kind of conversational space. In some sense this is what Berger (1969) meant when he described modern religion as existing in "sheltering enclaves."

But it is more. These are not enclaves with high walls, where the sacred world is kept pure and well-defended. Their ability to be powerful producers of sacred consciousness depends not just on their ability to evoke sacred reality

---

[4] This section follows closely the arguments developed in *Sacred Stories, Spiritual Tribes* (Ammerman 2013a).

in powerful ritual events or in coherent explanations of the cosmos. Rather, their power as sacred culture producers is in the degree to which they allow sacred and profane to intermingle. The people with the most robust sense of sacred presence in everyday life are not simply those who participate frequently, but those who engage in religious activities that allow for conversation and relationship. The conversations they engage inside the religious community are inevitably full of the stuff of everyday life, with mundane and sacred realities intermingling, and that mixture is part of what makes those conversations portable. Congregations gain their potency as producers of sacred consciousness not through their exclusivity or high boundaries, but as they create spaces for and encourage opportunities to imagine and speak about everyday realities among spiritual compatriots.

When people step beyond their religious communities, of course, they encounter an enormously plural and functionally complex modern world. People move through life with a shifting cast of characters in a shifting array of institutional settings. The primary mode of discourse and interaction in much of that world is likely to present itself as very this-worldly and non-spiritual. The task is to get the plane built or get the politician elected or measure out the right doses of medicine. Berger is right that the dominant reality mode is a secular one that we assume others can share and that allows us to proceed on common reality grounds. However, in nearly every social arena, there may be forms of spiritual community and conversation infusing the ongoing mundane work. The characters with whom we share the stage are not neatly compartmentalized, and narratives from one part of life are drawn on and refashioned across those domains, wherever there are social spaces in which religious and spiritual assumptions enter the conversation. One spiritually inclined person discovers another such person, and they start to talk.

People of faith seem, in fact, to have a knack for finding each other. We may not be surprised to find that roughly three-quarters of household partners share a common religious affiliation, but it is surprising that two-thirds of work-based friendships were described to us as religiously homogeneous—not necessarily people sharing exactly the same religious tradition, but people who think of each other as religiously similar. And in those religiously similar work friendships, people were more likely to report that they talk about religion.

What I am suggesting here is that religious identities can be part of the package of cultural cues that constitute the ever-shifting "tribes" of modern society (Maffesoli 1995), the signals by which we recognize each other. Some cues, distinctive dress perhaps, may make apparent that the participants come from a particular religious tradition. Some religious cues may divide and alienate people who are otherwise sharing the same (otherwise non-religious) social space.

Much of recent anxiety about "religion and public life" comes from exactly this fear that difference is being unnecessarily introduced into a space that would better be left neutral. In other instances, however, the commonality of social space and focus may create a bridge that allows religious differences to be mediated (Warner 1997). What people share in common may create a sufficient social bond to allow religious differences to be accommodated—but only if those differences are, in fact, recognized to be present. Recall what Putnam and Campbell (2010) found in their research: When people gain a new friend who is religiously different, they feel more friendly toward that religious group as a whole. So long as the friend remains a religiously anonymous co-worker, however, no religious bridging occurs. Secularizing all shared spaces may not be the most efficient strategy for a religiously tolerant society.

There are cautions, however. Bridging is seriously inhibited to the extent that religious communities do become insular, limiting the religious churn that makes friendly contact and common work normative. Peaceful coexistence is also threatened when religious identities are mobilized for divisive political purposes. Especially since the 1990s in the US, religious identities and political identities have been increasingly aligned, with an increasingly wide chasm between left and right (Putnam and Campbell 2010; Green, Rozell, and Wilcox 2003). Prior to the revolutions of the 1960s, denominational preference was much more likely to be influenced by social class position than by political party. Today, political cues are part of the cultural identity present in many local congregations. People choose where to belong, or not to belong at all, based in part on the political messages they see and hear in a congregation (Hout and Fischer 2002; Bean 2009). The conversations in local religious communities have become, then, part of the political echo chamber that keeps too many Americans from encountering, conversing with, and working alongside people who are outside their own political tribe.

In other parts of the world, barriers to interaction across religious lines are often much higher, even written into law and enforced by violence. As Berger points out in this book, religious identities are often made salient by politically divisive rhetoric, reinforcing loyalties and animosities. Whether attacking Rohingya Muslims in Buddhist Burma or slaughtering victims on either side of the Christian-Muslim divides in the Central African Republic, leaders bent on violently seizing power seem quite willing and able to convince followers that there is a sacred reality at the heart of their armed struggle. Ignoring that religious dimension would be foolish, even as it would be equally foolish to understand the conflict as solely the product of religious belief and fervor. Again, the sacred and the secular are intertwined.

Even when the question is not one of political violence, the dilemmas of managing the presence and multiplicity of religious consciousness are every bit as complicated as Berger's astute overview reveals. In schools, workplaces, and politics, various combinations of enforced secularity, laissez-faire mixing, and religious rules can be seen around the globe. The hijab has become something of a universal site of contestation in these experiments (AlSayyad and Castells 2002; Read and Bartkowski 2000). Is it required or forbidden, chosen or ignored? In places where there is legal and cultural room to choose, otherwise rather nontraditional women may wear hijab as a proud marker of their solidarity with a community to which they belong. In other places, where there are religious rules but some cultural flexibility, they may don endless varieties of stylish coverings that may or may not conform to strict tradition. In still other places, legal restrictions may make the hijab a political symbol as much as a religious one. Narratives of sacred consciousness intertwine with narratives of citizenship, politics, and individual autonomy.

Wherever that veiled Muslim goes, however, she introduces the reality that not everything is governed by modern reason, secular efficiency, and pluralist neutrality. When she wears her hijab under a hard hat or laboratory goggles or a graduation cap, she stands as a visible reminder that sacred and secular can exist side by side. In the world of everyday life, sacred stories can be found, for good and ill, throughout the social world. There is much more for scholars to learn about how and to what effect sacred consciousness intertwines with mundane realities. Sacred consciousness is produced both in institutionalized spiritual traditions and religious communities and in the shifting situational bonds of conversation among people who recognize their spiritual common ground (even if their specific beliefs and traditions may be different). In the modern world, there is no single social location in which to look for religion, nor is there a single shape in which we will find sacred consciousness. Recognizing the permeability of the boundaries between social spheres and between traditions is a major theoretical advance, taking us far beyond the secularization paradigm of old. Peter Berger's own rethinking of that earlier theory is a critical conceptual contribution to the important work of understanding a world full of sacred things.

References

AlSayyad, Nezar, and Manuel Castells, eds. 2002. *Muslim Europe or Euro-Islam: Politics, Culture, and Citizenship in the Age of Globalization*. Berkeley, Cal.: University of California Press.

Ammerman, Nancy T. 1994. "Telling Congregational Stories." *Review of Religious Research* 35 (4): 289–301.

——. 1997a. *Congregation and Community*. New Brunswick, NJ: Rutgers University Press.

——. 1997b. "Golden Rule Christianity: Lived Religion in the American Mainstream." In *Lived Religion in America: Toward a History of Practice*, edited by David Hall, 196–216. Princeton: Princeton University Press.

——. 1997c. "Religious Choice and Religious Vitality: The Market and Beyond." In *Assessing Rational Choice Models of Religion*, edited by Laurence A. Young, 119–132. New York: Routledge.

——. 2003. "Religious Identities and Religious Institutions." In *Handbook of the Sociology of Religion*, edited by Michele Dillon, 207–224. Cambridge: Cambridge University Press.

——. 2005a. *Pillars of Faith: American Congregations and Their Partners*. Berkeley, Cal.: University of California Press.

——. 2005b. "Religious Narratives, Community Service, and Everyday Public Life." In *Taking Faith Seriously*, edited by Mary Jo Bane, Brent Coffin and Richard Higgins, 146–174. Cambridge, Mass.: Harvard University Press.

——. ed. 2006. *Everyday Religion: Observing Modern Religious Lives*. New York: Oxford University Press.

——. 2013a. *Sacred Stories, Spiritual Tribes: Finding Religion in Everyday Life*. New York: Oxford University Press.

——. 2013b. "Spiritual but not Religious?: Beyond Binary Choices in the Study of Religion." *Journal for the Scientific Study of Religion* 52 (2): 258–278.

Asad, Talal. 1993. *Genealogies of Religion: Discipline and Reasons of Power in Christianity and Islam*. Baltimore, Md.: Johns Hopkins University Press.

Bean, Lydia Nan. 2009. *The Politics of Evangelical Identity in the United States and Canada*. Dissertation, Sociology, Harvard University, Cambridge, Mass.

Bellah, Robert N. 2011. *Religion in Human Evolution: From the Paleolithic to the Axial Age*. Cambridge, Mass.: Harvard University Press.

Bender, Courtney, Wendy Cadge, Peggy Levitt, and David A. Smilde, eds. 2012. *Religion on the Edge: De-Centering and Re-Centering the Sociology of Religion*. New York: Oxford University Press.

Berger, Peter L. 1969. *The Sacred Canopy*. Garden City, New York: Anchor Doubleday.

——. ed. 1999. *The Desecularization of the World: Resurgent Religion and World Politics*. Grand Rapids, Mich.: Eerdmans.

Berger, Peter L., and Thomas Luckmann. 1967. *The Social Construction of Reality*. Garden City, New York: Doubleday Anchor.

Bourdieu, Pierre. 1991. *Language and Symbolic Power*. Cambridge, Mass.: Harvard University Press.

Butler, Jon. 1990. *Awash in a Sea of Faith*. Cambridge, Mass.: Harvard University Press.

Chaves, Mark, and David E. Cann. 1992. "Regulation, Pluralism, and Religious Market Structure: Explaining Religion's Vitality." *Rationality and Society* 4 (3): 272–290.

Douglas, Mary. 1983. "The Effects of Modernization on Religious Change." In *Religion and America*, edited by Mary Douglas and Steven M. Tipton, 25–43. Boston: Beacon.

Du Bois, W. E. B. 1903 [2003]. *The Negro Church: Report of a Social Study Made under the Direction of Atlanta University*. Walnut Creek, Cal.: AltaMira.

Ebaugh, Helen Rose, and Janet Saltzman Chafetz. 1999. "Agents for Cultural Reproduction and Structural Change: The Ironic Role of Women in Immigrant Religious Institutions." *Social Forces* 78 (2): 585–613.

Ecklund, Elaine Howard. 2005. "Models of Civic Responsibility: Korean Americans in Congregations with Different Ethnic Compositions." *Journal for the Scientific Study of Religion* 44 (1): 15–28.

Emerson, Michael O. and Karen Chai Kim. 2003. "Multiracial Congregations: An Analysis of Their Development and a Typology." *Journal for the Scientific Study of Religion* 42 (2): 217–228.

Finke, Roger, and Rodney Stark. 1988. "Religious Economies and Sacred Canopies: Religious Mobilization in American Cities." *American Sociological Review* 53: 41–49.

Foley, Michael W., and Dean Hoge. 2007. *Religion and the New Immigrants: How Faith Communities Form Our Newest Citizens*. New York: Oxford University Press.

Fraser, Nancy. 1990. "Rethinking the Public Sphere: A Contribution to the Critique of Actually Existing Democracy." *Social Text* 25 (26): 56–80.

Friedland, Roger, and Robert R. Alford. 1991. "Bringing Society Back In: Symbols, Practices, and Institutional Contradictions." In *The New Institutionalism in Organizational Analysis*, edited by W. Powell and P. DiMaggio, 232–263. Chicago: University of Chicago Press.

Green, John C., Mark J. Rozell, and Clyde Wilcox., eds. 2003. *The Christian Right in American Politics: Marching to the Millennium*. Washington, D.C.: Georgetown University Press.

Hall, David, ed. 1997. *Lived Religion in America*. Princeton: Princeton University Press.

Hatch, Nathan G. 1989. *The Democratization of American Christianity*. New Haven: Yale University Press.

Hout, Michael, and Claude Fischer. 2002. "Why More Americans Have No Religious Preference: Politics and Generations." *American Sociological Review* 67: 165–190.

Iannaccone, Laurence R. 1991. "The Consequences of Religious Market Structure: Adam Smith and the Economics of Religion." *Rationality and Society* 3 (2): 156–177.

Kurien, Prema A. 2007. *A Place at the Multicultural Table: The Development of an American Hinduism*. New Brunswick, NJ: Rutgers University Press.

Lincoln, C. Eric, and Lawrence H. Mamiya. 1990. *The Black Church in the African American Experience*. Durham, NC: Duke University Press.

McGuire, Meredith B. 2008. *Lived Religion: Faith and Practice in Everyday Life*. New York: Oxford University Press.

Maffesoli, Michel. 1995. *The Time of Tribes*. Beverly Hills, Cal.: Sage.

Mooney, Margarita. 2009. *Faith Makes Us Live: Surviving and Thriving in the Haitian Diaspora*. Berkeley, Cal.: University of California Press.

Munson, Ziad. 2006. "When A Funeral Isn't Just A Funeral: The Layered Meaning Of Everyday Action." In *Everyday Religion: Observing Modern Religious Lives*, edited by Nancy T. Ammerman, 121–136. New York: Oxford University Press.

Olson, Daniel V. A. 1999. "Religious Pluralism and U.S. Church Membership: A Reassessment." *Sociology of Religion* 60 (2): 149–173.

Putnam, Robert D., and David E. Campbell. 2010. *American Grace: How Religion Divides and Unites Us*. New York: Simon & Schuster.

Read, Jen'nan Ghazal, and John Bartkowski. 2000. "To Veil or not to Veil? A Case Study of Identity Negotiation among Muslim Women in Austin, Texas." *Gender and Society* 14 (3): 395–417.

Somers, Margaret R. 1994. "The Narrative Constitution of Identity: A Relational and Network Approach." *Theory and Society* 23: 605 – 649.

Taylor, Charles. 2007. *A Secular Age*. Cambridge, Mass.: Belknap Press.

Warner, R. Stephen. 1993. "Work in Progress toward a New Paradigm for the Sociological Study of Religion in the United States." *American Journal of Sociology* 98 (5): 1044 – 93.

——. 1997. "Religion, Boundaries, and Bridges." *Sociology of Religion* 58 (3): 217 – 238.

——. 1999. "Changes in the Civic Role of Religion." In *Diversity and Its Discontents: Cultural Conflict and Common Ground in Contermporary American Society*, edited by Neil J. Smelser and Jeffrey C. Alexander, 229 – 243. Princeton: Princeton University Press.

Weber, Max. 1958 [1930]. *The Protestant Ethic and the Spirit of Capitalism*. Translated by T. Parsons. New York: Scribner.

Response by Detlef Pollack: Toward a New Paradigm for the Sociology of Religion?

Translated from the German by Ruth Pauli

Peter L. Berger is one of the few sociologists of religion in our time who has not only made contributions at the highest level of scientific discourse, but who, during the past decades, has also codetermined its profile to a high degree. His religious-sociological oeuvre of the 1960s and 1970s set the tone for the then-predominant approach– the secularization theory. To this day, some exponents of the secularization theory, such as Steve Bruce or Frank Lechner, are influenced by him. All work done since then in the field of sociology of religion has been strongly affected by his thesis that religious concepts and practices gain their stability from the surrounding plausibility structure shared by the majority, and that their acceptance is eroded by the growing pluralism of religious options. It is no exaggeration to suggest that the economic market paradigm, even though it explicitly distinguishes itself from secularization theory, nonetheless also deals with this thesis.[1] In the judgement of Rodney Stark and his colleagues, the vitality of religion is not weakened but enhanced by the competition of various religious providers. They reverse Berger's argument: Where a single religious group holds a monopolistic position, it loses attractiveness; where many religious groups compete for the favor of religious consumers, the general level of religiousness is on the rise (Stark/Finke 2000).

Yet, it was not this argument that caused Peter L. Berger to abandon his position on secularization theory during the 1990's. Even after having recanted it, he still holds to his theory of undermining – the claim that growing plurality in the religious field undermines the social validity of religious convictions and withdraws their plausibility, which is taken for granted as long as these convictions are shared by the majority. As early as 2001, in a work edited by Linda Woodhead which discusses Berger's oeuvre both with criticism and with appreciation, he says: "I would say, I was wrong about secularization, but right about pluralism... What pluralism does...is to undermine all taken-for-granted certainties, in religion as in all other spheres of life" (Berger 2001: 194). In reality, it was not the competing hypothesis of market theoreticians that made him abandon the theory of secularization. Rather, it was the understanding of the unbroken

---

1 This is suggested by the arguments of Stephen Warner who, in his 1993 essay, attributed to market theory the status of a new paradigm. He explicitly identified the old paradigm with the early oeuvre of Peter Berger (Warner 1993: 1045).

vitality of religion, which, as he claimed, is as strong today as ever and is undiminished even by the undoubtedly dramatic changes brought about by modernization, technologization, and rationalization. "Religion has not been declining. On the contrary, in much of the world there has been a veritable explosion of religious faith" (Berger 2008: 23). Western Europe and the globally active cultural and intellectual elites could count as examples of religion's loss of importance. However, they might both be exceptions in an otherwise passionately religious world. Berger considers the rise of Islam and the growth of dynamic Evangelicalism (especially in its Pentacostal version) as the most impressive evidence for what he diagnoses as religious explosion. His repudiation of secularization theory was induced, above all, by these religious risings.

One cannot but admire such intellectual radicalism and significance, when the leading exponent of a theory is willing to abandon it because, in his opinion, it proves to be wrong in the light of new empirical evidence. Such scientific honesty exists only rarely among members of the scientific community.

In his newly published text, however, Peter L. Berger once more modifies his position, proclaiming it with a fair amount of caution, contrary to his earlier theory, even with the caveat that his new ideas might one day be proven false. But even then, the fact that he has yet again corrected his course proves at least one thing: even in his old age, the master has not lost his intellectual flexibility. Now, almost twenty years later, Berger states that the theory which he then abandoned because he considered it untenable might not have been as wrong as he previously thought (p. XII). This is to say that modernity – exactly as the secularization theory claims – has indeed produced a secular discourse that enables people to deal with many areas of life without reference to any religious interpretations of reality (p. 51). This discourse is to be found not only in Western Europe or among intellectual elites, but also among ordinary believers all over the world. According to Berger, the theoreticians of secularity have made the mistake of assigning an exclusive position to this discourse and underestimating the capacity of people to live in different realms of reality – religious and secular – and to switch between them (p. 53). This mistake has even occured among the critics of the secularization theory. For the majority of people, faith and secularity are not mutually exclusive modes of attending to reality but are complementary approaches to reality whose relation is not a matter of "either/or," but rather of "both/and." Thus it is not possible, in his estimation, to simply replace the secularization theory with the thesis of a return of the gods: It would be as senseless to uphold secularization theory in view of the vital religiousness in a modernizing world as to negate the plausibility of the evolution of an *imma-*

nent frame, which is neutral towards religion.[2] As to secularization theory, the insight was correct that an influential secular discourse had developed, which joined the religious discourse and even enjoyed a privileged position in society as well as in the minds of individuals. But it was wrong to assume that the secular discourse had pushed aside the religious worldview and could now have complete dominance over definitions of reality and value orientations. In contrast to the assumptions of secularization theory, modernization has not inevitably led to a complete secularization of society. Rather, the inevitable consequence of modernity has been the pluralization of worldviews and value systems. Following Berger, modernity thereby produces two kinds of pluralism: on the one hand, religious pluralism, consisting of a diversity of different religious traditions; and on the other hand, a pluralism of religious and secular discourses. Since both society and individuals are shaped by these discourses, the consequences of modernity underlying pluralization mold not only society but also the minds of individuals.[3] Thus Berger postulates a correlation between pluralization on the level of society, expressing itself in the differentiation of institutions such as science, administration, medicine, or technology, and the pluralization of individual consciousness (p. 35). Such a correlation, in his view, does not have to lead to complete accordance, but only to a certain mutual dependence.

In stating as much, Berger does not attempt to revoke his recantation of secularization theory; he merely changes it. It is not an about-face. You might call it a 90-degree turn. What do we gain from this course correction?

---

2 In stating as much, Berger adopts the argument of Charles Taylor (2007), though not without criticizing the book's title, "A Secular Age," as misleading; one could describe our age as being pluralist rather than secular (p. 73).

3 Berger already assumed that social and mental changes corresponded. This thesis of correspondance distinguished his position from that of Thomas Luckmann, who, like Berger, assumed the differentiation and secularization of the social structure and the system of institutions once modern societies evolve, but always negated quite incomprehensibly a secularization of the individual mind. The churches' loss of relevance in society as a result of institutional specialization would not lead inevitably to an individual loss of faith en masse, Luckmann argued (1972: 11). Even when chuches lose their anchoring in the holy cosmos and social institutions become increasingly secular, the individual stays religious (Luckmann 1991: 147 f.). Berger, however, does not exempt the individual consciousness from the process of secularization: "As there is a secularization of society and culture, so there is a secularization of consciousness. Put simply, this means that the modern West has produced an increasing number of individuals who look upon the world and their own lives without the benefit of religious interpretations" (Berger 1969: 107 f.).

First of all, Berger makes it clear that his abandoning of the presuppositions of secularization theory does not mean its reversal.[4] He does not plead for a theory of sacralization or resacralization. Modernity has secularizing effects, but they are limited (p. 76-77). Above all, they exist in the emergence of an immanent pattern of interpreting the world, which penetrates many social spheres, scientific analysis, jurisdiction, economic action, and also everyday life. Nonetheless, worlds of religious concepts, finite provinces of meaning, and rituals can cetainly hold their ground. That is the very meaning of the pluralism of worldviews.

Further, Berger does not adopt the concept of a necessary interdependence between the constitutional conditions of modernity and the processes of secularization. Thus he takes into account an oft-repeated critcism of secularization theory.[5] Modernity does not inevitably bring forth secularization; neither does it lead to the ultimate disappearance of religion. Berger avoids any deterministic or teleological overtone. In fact, the interdependence of modernity and the emergence of a secular discourse is to be understood historically. This opens up the way to an empirical examination of the historically variable preconditions of the origin of this interdependence. One of the theories implicit in Berger's considerations might be that religious pluralism itself, being distinctive of modernity, has contributed to the emergence of a secular discourse because all of the conflicts resulting from the diversification of the religious, as they were fought out in the confessional wars of the 16th and 17th centuries, could only be solved by creating a religiously neutral realm, as Berger remarks.

If Berger is indeed right that the pluralization of worldviews and value systems is the central signum of our age, then the secularization approach, being above all an identification of the interdependence of religion and modernity, could be overcome – as is often demanded and attempted. This could be most effectively done by intensely debating the phenomenon of the pluralization of

---

4 That is what some sociologists of religion tend to do when trying to overthrow the secularization theory – for example, José Casanova not only observes deprivatization of religion contradicting secularization theory (Casanova 1994), but also denies, in his more recent works, the close connection of differentiation and secularization stated by secularization theory and instead emphasizes the contribution of religion to the evolution of modernity. In these works he even goes so far as to invert the underlying values of secularization theory: He replaces the modern esteem of Enlightenment and reason with an emphatic appreciation of Catholicism, and he replaces the criticism of religion with a criticism of European civilization as being intolerant, violent, and unreflected (Casanova 2008a, 2008b). For more details, see Pollack (2009: 5f.).
5 Critics of the deterministic, teleological, and unilinear character of the theory of secularization include Hans Joas (2007), Ulrich Beck (2008), Grace Davie (2002), and Danièle Hervieu-Léger (2000).

worldview and religion. This debate has the potential to inherit the predominance once held by the theory of secularization. In that case, various questions will have to be discussed, such as the emergence of two pluralisms, their relationship to each other, the conditions for a co-existence of secular and religious discourse, and also their consequences and the ways to handle them in law, politics, and society. Also important is yet another question – What other relations between religious and secular discourse are imaginable and likely, apart from their co-existence: mutual exclusion, conflict, predominance of one over the other, subversion, mutual penetration, provincialization, isolation, persistence, revolutionary universalization? Furthermore, the discussion of the social, political, and jurisdictional conditions of different constellations and types of plurality, of the relationship of individual consciousness and social institutions as well as of culture and social structure, could be of interest. Berger's approach, based on pluralism theory, is undoubtedly a promising research agenda, which, though it still needs to be elaborated and developed, already proves stimulating in multiple ways. In spite of this potential, Berger's approach brings up critical questions that merit some discussion.

There are three issues that remain unconvincing in Peter L. Berger's reasoning as presented in this book. Firstly, it is difficult to comprehend whether in this new book Berger is actually still distancing himself from his earlier secularization theory. The core of Berger's earlier approach, based on secularization theory, was the assumption that religious homogeneity enhances the taken-for-granted validity of individual religious concepts and practices, and that religious diversity, on the other hand, undermines it. Berger still adheres to the theory of undermining: pluralism, he states, relativizes and undermines certainties (p. 10); by depriving religion of its taken-for-granted quality, pluralism fosters secularity (p. 20). Berger no longer holds the view that modernization necessarily leads to secularization (p. 20). According to Berger, this assumption is no longer acceptable in the light of developments in the technologically highly modernized USA or the modernizing states of Latin America and Asia, where an "explosion of passionate religious movements" is a prominent feature.[6] At the same time, he still claims in this new text that modernity and pluralism are inexorably intertwined: "modernity necessarily leads to pluralism" (p. 20). Today, pluralism is ubiquitous. In modernity, he says, people are increasingly exposed to the competition of differing convictions, values, and lifestyles. However, if modernization inevitably provokes pluralization, and pluralization undermines religious

---

6 There is a similar argument in Berger's previous work (2008: 10).

certainties, the consequence must be that modernization is accompanied by a weakening of religious convictions. This proposition is the core of any secularization theory. Berger will have to make a decision between abandoning the secularization theory or adhering to the theorem of undermining. Only if he also decided to abandon the theorem of undermining would he truly overcome secularization theory. But this he does not want to do; he cannot dispense with the theorem of undermining because it is at the core of his religious-sociological approach. This leads us to the conclusion that Berger, involuntarily, is much more committed to the secularization theory than he is ready to admit. His turn is probably greater than the assumed 90 degrees. Berger has abandoned the assumption that all processes attributed to modernity, whether rationalization, technolgization, or the penetration of science in all spheres, minimize the importance of religion. But he has not abandonned – at least in his theoretical argumentation – the assumed necessity of the three steps leading from modernization to pluralization and finally to secularization.

However, this context of argumentation – which evidently is theoretically imposed, though not intended by Berger – raises another question: How does his theory of undermining relate to his claim that one can observe an explosion of religious faith all over the world, which would undeniably be accompanied by a pluralization of the religious field? Is Rodney Stark's economic market theory, according to which religious competition would increase the level of religiousness, correct after all? In order to settle this question, further reflection and empirical analysis are required.[7] Religiously diversified societies are probably especially religiously productive when their immanent religious pluralism is embedded in an all-embracing religious consensus in which it is mitigated and integrated. In a religiously saturated country like the USA, where practically everybody believes in God and is convinced that there is a life after death in which you are punished or rewarded for your earthly deeds, religious competition may inspire religious enthusiasm; in countries like the Netherlands or Great Britain, however, where the level of religious plurality is also very high but a strong religious framing is lacking, it might have a paralysing rather than a stimulating effect.

If this hypothesis contained even a grain of truth, you could perhaps reconcile Stark's market model with Berger's theory of undermining. In that case, you

---

7 There are already innumerable studies of the effects of religious pluralism on the level of religiousness. See the following authors, who hold to the economic market model: Stark/Finke (2000), Iannaccone (1992, 1994), and Froese/Pfaff (2001). The contrary position is held by Lechner (1996, 2004), Dobbelaere (2002), and Bruce (2002, 2011). An overview of the literature is offered in Olson (2008).

could possibly make the following generalization: Under the conditions of a so-ciety-wide religious consensus – even if very weak in content – religious compe-tition increases religious enthusiasm, stimulates the religious "providers" to in-tensify their commitment, and stimulates the religious consumers to intensly search for the best "offer." Given the cultural context, it is evident that everyone is following a religious preference – it just depends on where one thinks one's religious needs are best satisfied. Under the conditions of a majoritarian secular culture, the plurality of different religious communities and interpretations of meaning is not effective in inspiring and motivating, but rather in relativizing and restricting. In this respect, Berger's theory of the "heretical imperative" should perhaps be reconsidered. It is possible that the imperative to chose exists only in societies where being religious is taken for granted, no matter what form that might take. However, it seems to be very likely that in a widely secularized society many do not make a religious choice at all, leaving the question of the truth of faith untouched. In such a society, one needs no religion at all and does not have to decide on religious matters.

The second objection refers to Berger's thesis of the co-existence of religious and secular discourse. Taking up the concepts of the finite provinces of meaning and the paramount reality – developed in the 1950s by Peter L. Berger's teacher Alfred Schütz – Berger proposes that there are different finite provinces of mean-ing in human consciousness that can co-exist. In the same way one returns from the reality of a theater production (Berger's example, p. 55) back to the reality of everyday life, and then leaves it again for, say, mathematical speculations, it should be possible to use different secular and religious codes and semantics, and to switch from one to the other. I will call this Berger's compatibility theory. But is it possible to differentiate between secular and religious discourses by their semantic and mundane relevance structure in the same way as one differ-entiates between mathematical and aesthetic discourses or between erotic and political communications? A woman can be erotically attractive to a man, when on the occasion of a political discussion he discovers her beauty – to quote another of Berger's examples. Her erotic attractiveness might even grow once the man discovers that they both share the same political convictions. How-ever, it might also grow – and this is the end of the analogy to Berger's example – when they find out that their political opinions are completely different. And it is possible that his desire does not depend at all on her political views. Political and erotic relevance structures can easily be distinguished, and sometimes it is wise (for the sake of love) not to relate them too closely.

There is no absolute guarantee that it is possible to differentiate between secular and religious discourses. Whether God is the world's ultimate goal or life is without ultimate purpose, whether you believe in miracles or deny their possibility, whether you believe that you need ritual practice and prayers to obtain happiness and salvation or you think that people forge their own destinies, these alternatives are hardly compatible. Erotic and political discourses belong to different worlds of meaning without necessarily influencing each other. In the case of religious and secular discourses, and even more so in the case of different religious discourses, there is a high probability that they compete against each other. This probability grows the more religions lay claim to a universal interpretation of the world, because in this case the probability of a mutual overlapping of the discourses also grows. Then they act in the same medium: in the medium of truth. The proposition that the dead will rise is not compatible with the proposition that death puts an end to everything; the belief in Jesus Christ as God's incarnation is not compatible with the belief that God is so different from anything earthly that God could never become a human being; the conviction that the Bible is true in its literal sense does not allow for historical-critical interpretation.[8]

Berger is aware of this objection. Does not religion, he asks (p. 58), claim an overall relevance which embraces all the others? Does not religion – as Paul Tillich wrote – embody "the ultimate concern" to which every other concern is secondary? Berger responds to this objection by opening up a differentiation of time: It may be that the ultimate concerns imply an overall relevance, the whole of human existence, the cosmos; however, this does not preclude that we put away the ultimate concerns for a while in order to attend to more mundane ones. To do so does not mean that the ultimate dimension is diminished or denied, but simply that at the moment we are occupied with other things. But are paramount reality and God's reality with its ultimate relevance really free of tension? Is it not possible that the everyday world fascinates us to such an extent that we gradually lose interest in the afterworld? In the perception of the everyday world, don't we follow a different logic than in the religious field? Does the everyday world not suggest a definition of reality that conflicts in both a hidden and an open way with the religious worldview, with all its assumptions about the

---

8 To make the point even clearer, it should be noted that the tensions between religious and secular worldviews described here are of merely modal character. They might occur, but not of necessity. It is absolutely conceivable that while attending a religious service or in a comparable situation, people use a religious code to communicate, whereas under different circumstances, like in their work surroundings, they use the secular code, and still they do not have the notion that these two forms of communication are contradictory. However, since many religions raise the claim of universality, there is a higher probability that religious discourses come into conflict with scientific, erotic, or political discourses than that erotic and scientific discourses, for instance, are at odds with each other.

beginning and end of the world, about the salvation of the world and human-kind? These questions become even more aggravating when one supposes, as Berger does, that secularized discourse enjoys a privileged status. In this case, the secular side's questions about the religious interpretations of the world will become all the more pressing.

Naturally, one can deal with concepts of salvation and the fate of the world that differ from one's own beliefs on a cognitive level – by downgrading them. When in the 19th century there was a mass immigration of Irish Catholics to Scotland, the Scottish Presbyterians did not have to question their faith. They could keep at a distance the Catholic faith of the Irish immigrants by developing demeaning stereotypes about them and by portraying them as uncultured, un-disciplined idlers devoted to alcohol (Bruce 2001: 93). Berger and Luckmann call this process of handling definitions of reality differing from one's own sym-bolic universe "neutralization," meaning "assigning an inferior ontological sta-tus...to all definitions existing outside the symbolic universe" (Berger/Luckmann 1966: 133). The neutralization results from either disqualifying the competing def-inition of reality from the discourse or subordinating it to one's own worldview, allowing that it might be partially true. If in fact you treat secular communica-tion—influenced by science, technology, and politics—as privileged discourse, as Berger does, then you attribute to the religious discourses at best the status of a secondary language, which, on the part of primary codes and relevances, will be under the constant pressure of justification. It is not discernible how such a secondary language competing with the primary one can reach persisten-cy and co-existence with the primary code without being challenged, and some-day perhaps even overpowered, by the latter.

Berger finds his way out of this dilemma by arguing that the pluralism of dis-courses affects only the "how" of faith – that one has to live in a world with dif-ferent definitions of reality and, therefore, any supposition about reality is rid-dled with doubt but does not affect the "what" of faith (p. 32). The content of faith, he says, does not change in the light of the plurality of competing systems of values and convictions, even if the "how" of faith has radically changed its character through experiencing this plurality. This argument is hardly convinc-ing, as the contents of faith cannot so easily be detached from their form.

This brings me to my third objection. Empirical religious-sociological re-search has shown that in countries with a growing religious plurality, the con-tents of faith become increasingly vague, diffuse, and indetermined (Pollack 2009). In Western Europe (and, incidentally, also in the USA) there is a growing segment of people who no longer believe that the Bible is the word of God that has to be understood literally, but that it merely contains certain religious or es-sential life truths. A growing number of Western Europeans no longer imagine

God as a person, but as a higher power. On the question of life after death, they do not reflect in Christian terms by associating it with the ressurection of the dead or even of the flesh, but rather by adopting common concepts including the notion of the immortal soul, a belief in Heaven, or a belief in reincarnation. Above all, one implication of the growing plurality of the religious sphere is that the contents of faith become indetermined, and another is that, because it is impossible to make a choice between the many competing propositions of faith, one becomes increasingly indifferent about faith and leaves the query about truth unanswered. Holding on to the contents of one's faith despite increasing religious pluralism seems rather a minority position, found above all in closed communities. Religious concepts are especially distinguished by a high degree of plasticity. Perhaps no other sphere of society is as sensible to surroundings as the religious one.

Berger's considerations on religious pluralism prove to be stimulating. They take up traditional questions concerning the sociology of religion, such as the relation between religion and modernity, and they open up new perspectives for research. The classical thesis of the modernization theory is superseded by Berger's propositions on the theory of pluralism. The assertion that modernity necessarily leads to secularization is replaced by the presupposition that modernity inevitably comes along with a pluralism of religions and worldviews. This allows Berger to dissociate himself convincingly from the old theories of secularization, which posit a relation between rationalization, industrialization, urbanization, and secularization. At the same time, he is able to hold on to the repeatedly confirmed correlation between modernity and pluralization. Basically, Berger ascribes to a paradigm of differentiation theory,[9] which not only acts on the assumption of a pluralism of different religious orientations, but also assumes a pluralism of religious and secular discourses, which results from the former.

It has become clear that this approach is heavily biased toward a strengthening of the secularization theory, albeit in a fresh garment. This assumption is confirmed by the fact that, in the end, it turns out to be a differentiation theory, because in this assumed differentiation of religion and the secular, of religion and politics, of religion and science, or of religion and morals, many social scientists see the analytical core of the secularization theory (see Pollack 2013). Another proof for this assumption is Berger's argument that pluralism, as a feature

---

9 Not by accident Berger writes (p. 57): "This differentiation of reality into multiple relevance structures is a key feature of modernity, ultimately grounded in the immensely broad increase in the division of labor. If one wants, one can call the process secularization."

inseparable from modernity, has the effect of undermining the certainties of religious concepts. This argument is not compatible with the proposition of an undiminished religious vitality all over the world, assuming that the world is growing increasingly interconnected. This is also accompanied by the acceptance of partially secularizing effects of modernity when forming an *immanent frame*. The secular discourse, especially when enjoying a privileged status, puts growing plausibility pressure on the religious discourse. As Berger says, it is granted that religious and secular codes can co-exist. Nonetheless, they can be in a tenuous relation, which is often precisely the case. Finally, the compatibility of religion and secularity assumed by Berger is also endangered because, with the increasing plurality of worldviews and religions, not only the forms but also the contents of faith are changing, and – not least for the sake of their comapatibility with secular defintions of reality – are becoming increasingly diffuse, common, and vague. All of these elements are strengthening the well-known assumptions of secularization theory.

Considering as much, should Peter L. Berger not decide to emphazise secularization theory in his future work more than he has already done in this book? Even if religious and secular definitions of the world might co-exist, and, to an even greater extent, erotic and political discourses might co-exist; even if one is not compelled to make a choice between various religious options; in science "either/or" prevails over "both/and." In science, an acceptance of mutually exclusive statements cannot exist.

References

Beck, Ulrich. 2008. *Der eigene Gott: Von der Friedensfähigkeit und dem Gewaltpotential der Religionen*. Frankfurt a. M. / Leipzig: Verlag der Weltreligionen.

Berger, Peter L., and Thomas Luckmann. 1966. *The Social Construction of Reality*. London: Allen Lane.

Berger, Peter L. 1969. *The Sacred Canopy*. New York: Doubleday.

——. 2001. "Postscript." In *Peter Berger and the Study of Religion*, edited by Linda Woodhead, 189–198. London / New York: Routledge.

——. 2008. "Secularization Falsified." *First Things* 180: 23–28.

Bruce, Steve. 2001. "The curious case of an unnecessary recantation: Berger and secularization." In *Peter Berger and the Study of Religion*, edited by Linda Woodhead, 87–100. London / New York: Routledge.

——. 2002. *God is Dead: Secularization in the West*. Oxford: Blackwell.

——. 2011. *Secularization: In Defence of an Unfashionable Theory*. Oxford: Oxford University Press.

Casanova, José. 1994. *Public Religions in the Modern World*. Chicago: Chicago University Press.

——. 2008a. "Public Religions Revisited." In *Christentum und Solidarität: Bestandsaufnahmen zu Sozialethik und Religionssoziologie*, edited by Hermann Josef Große Kracht and Christian Spieß, 313–338. Paderborn u. a.: Schöningh.

——. 2008b. "The Problem of Religion and the Anxieties of European Secular Democracy." In *Religion and Democracy in Contemporary Europe*, edited by Gabriel Motzkin and Yochi Fischer, 63–74. Jerusalem: Alliance.

Dobbelaere, Karel. 2002. *Secularization: An Analysis at Three Levels*. Brüssel: Lang.

Davie, Grace. 2002. *Europe: The Exceptional Case: Parameters of Faith in the Modern World*. London: Darton, Longman and Todd.

Froese, Paul, and Steven Pfaff. 2001. "Replete and Desolate Markets: Poland, East Germany, and the New Religious Paradigm." *Social Forces* 80: 481–507.

Hervieu-Léger, Danièle. 2000. *Religion as a Chain of Memory*. Cambridge: Polity Press.

Iannaccone, Laurence. 1992. "Religious Market and the Economics of Religion." *Social Compass* 39: 123–131.

——. 1994. "Why Strict Churches Are Strong." *American Journal of Sociology* 99: 1180–1211.

Joas, Hans. 2007. "Führt Modernisierung zu Säkularisierung?" In *Woran glauben? Religion zwischen Kulturkampf und Sinnsuche*, edited by Gerd Nollmann and Hermann Strasser, 37–45. Essen: Klartext.

Lechner, Frank J. 1996. "Secularization in the Netherlands?" *Journal for the Scientific Study of Religion* 35: 252–264.

——. 2004. "Secularization." In *The Encyclopedia of Protestantism*, edited by Hans Joachim Hillerbrand, 1701–1707. New York / London: Routledge.

Luckmann, Thomas. 1972. "Religion in der modernen Gesellschaft." In *Religion im Umbruch: Soziologische Beiträge zur Situation von Religion und Kirche in der gegenwärtigen Gesellschaft*, edited by Jakobus Wössner, 3–15. Stuttgart: Enke.

——. 1991. *Die unsichtbare Religion*. Frankfurt a. M.: Suhrkamp. (Translation of Luckmann, Thomas, *The Invisible Religion: The Problem of Religion in Modern Society*, New York: Macmillan, 1967).

Olson, Daniel V. A. 2008. "Quantitative Evidence Favoring and Opposing the Religious Economies Model." In *The Role of Religion in Modern Societies*, edited by Detlef Pollack and Daniel V. A. Olson, 95–113. New York / London: Routledge.

Pollack, Detlef. 2009. *Rückkehr des Religiösen? Studien zum religiösen Wandel in Deutschland und Europa II*. Tübingen: Mohr.

——. 2013. "Secularization." In *Oxford Bibliographies*. URL: http://www.oxfordbibliographies. com/view/document/obo-9780199756384/obo-9780199756384-0073.xml?rskey= DHqVtF&result=83&q=

Stark, Rodney, and Roger Finke. 2000. *Acts of Faith: Explaining the Human Side of Religion*. Berkeley / Los Angeles: University of California Press.

Taylor, Charles. 2007. *A Secular Age*. Cambridge: Harvard University Press.

Warner, Stephen R. 1993. "Work in Progress Toward a New Paradigm for the Sociological Study of Religion in the United States." *American Journal of Sociology* 98: 1044–1093.

Response by Fenggang Yang:
Agency-Driven Secularization and Chinese Experiments in Multiple Modernities

In 1999, Peter Berger "very noisily" rescinded the secularization theory that he formulated in the 1960s. Since then, he has reiterated this retraction on many occasions, both in his writings and speeches and in speaking to sociologists of religion and to wider audiences of cultural and political elites in many countries. However, until now, some people in the intelligentsia, both in the East and the West, seem to hold a certain resentment about his rescindment and cling to the old paradigm thinking. For these people, Peter Berger's new book, *The Many Altars of Modernity: Toward a Paradigm for Religion in a Pluralist Age*, might look like a welcome course reversal. He takes a step back, trying to salvage some notions from his earlier theory in an effort to construct what he calls "a new paradigm." However, in my view, this is neither a new paradigm nor a revamping of the old theory, but rather a new theory of agency-driven secularization. In this theory, he offers new insights that are important for the theoretical development of the social scientific study of religion and religious pluralism in the modern world.

In order to move forward, however, it appears that we must first deal with some old issues associated with the paradigm shift. We also need to distinguish between descriptive and normative theories. Peter Berger's new theorizing is more of a normative theory than a descriptive theory, and such a theory may serve as the basis for an intentional secularization program. In fact, China, as a late-developing country, has experimented with various models of intentional secularization. The Chinese case demonstrates the need to assess the social consequences of various models instead of simply regarding them all as equally modern. Lastly, I will suggest some conceptual clarification of Berger's new insights for the purpose of theoretical construction in the social scientific study of religious pluralism.

Problems in the Paradigm Shift

First of all, I was initially puzzled by the title of Peter Berger's new text, which seems to suggest that this is the first-ever attempt to construct a new paradigm. However, to me, and probably to many other sociologists of religion as well, a new paradigm is already very well in place now. More than twenty years ago,

R. Stephen Warner (1993) published his seminal article, "Work in Progress Toward a New Paradigm for the Sociological Study of Religion in the United States," which made a comprehensive review of the massive literature accumulated for several decades and heralded the emergence of a new paradigm, "the crux of which is that organized religion thrives in the United States in an open market system, an observation anomalous to the older paradigm's monopoly concept" (p. 1044).

The old paradigm assumes the normality of a monopoly religion that functions as a "sacred canopy" over society and in which religious pluralism is perceived as fracturing the "sacred canopy." That is, when people of multiple faiths come to live in the same modernizing society, each faith system becomes inevitably relativized in its truth claims by the presence of other faiths. Over time, more and more people would lose their faith, and so religion is destined to wither away. Whereas the old paradigm perceives that religious pluralism erodes the plausibility structure of religion, thus leading to the relativization and decline of religion, the new paradigm sees religious pluralism as favorable for religious vitality. In short, the central dispute between the old and new paradigms is about the effect of religious pluralism.

About ten years after the initial herald, Warner (2002) recounted the further and rapid progress of the sociology of religion and declared that the new paradigm had spectacularly solidified and prevailed by then. This is the paradigm shift I have followed closely since my years of graduate study in the 1990s. Of course, within the new paradigm, there are various theories, including the subcultural identity and religious economy theories. The subcultural identity theory argues that people do not necessarily need the all-embracing "sacred canopy" of a monopoly religion; instead, "sacred umbrellas" in subcultural communities are sufficient for retaining religion in a modern society (Smith 1998). The religious economy theories argue that religious pluralism would engender competition in an open market, which in turn would tend to lead to higher religious participation (Stark and Finke 2000). I myself have joined the theoretical construction within the new paradigm by proposing a political economic approach to examining the demand-driven religious economy in China under Communist rule (Yang 2012).

A paradigm shift proves to be a painful process for some of the old-timers. In spite of the mounting empirical evidence of a worldwide religious persistence or resurgence, some people cling to the old paradigm through the back door of exceptionalism. At first, facing the empirical evidence of religious vitality in the United States, scholars working within the secularization paradigm resorted to American exceptionalism as an explanation. That is, the United States must be exceptional in going against the modern trend of all-encompassing secularization; it is only a matter of time until the United States begins to follow the norm of the modern world and see a religious decline. These people are eager to find any new sign of the decline of religion or religious significance in US society.

But an increasing number of empirical findings show that religion is not only persisting in the United States but is also persisting and resurging in many parts of the modern and modernizing world. Moreover, religion continues to play important public roles (e.g., Casanova 1988). Thus, some scholars of the old paradigm have proposed that perhaps it is Western Europe that is the exceptional case in its secularization. However, the secularization theory may not necessarily hold true for Europe either. Grace Davie's empirical studies (1994; 2000) find that the majority of Europeans have not lost their religious beliefs, although their church attendance is much lower than that of Americans. Davie describes the European religious situation as "believing without belonging." With the support of such empirical evidence, the new paradigm theorists have extended their theory to explaining the religious situation in Europe. According to Stark and associates (Stark and Iannaccone 1994; Stark and Finke 2000), the lower church attendance in Europe has nothing to do with the advanced modernity or modernization, nor does it prove the exception to the general pattern. Instead, it is a consequence of the religious regulations and the remnants of the state church in European societies. If deregulation occurs, free competition of plural religions will lead to greater religious participation. Some scholars have examined some empirical evidence to explain how this has happened in parts of Europe (e.g., Hamberg and Pettersson 1994).

Nevertheless, some scholars (see Berger, Davie and Fokas 2008) seem to be torn between the conflicting perceptions: Should the United States or should Europe be regarded as the exceptional case? Unsurprisingly, some people (e.g., Fan 2011) also argue for Chinese exceptionalism: Chinese religion and religiosity are so unique that no theory based on studies of Europe or the United States is suitable to explain China. As a response to such reactions in Europe and China, Stephen Warner reiterates his modest claim: The new paradigm would apply only to explain religion in the United States, whereas the secularization paradigm might be more suitable to explain religion in Europe. Following this logic, there would be different paradigms to explain religion in China, India, and other parts of the world. In an interview published by the Chinese newspaper *China Ethnic News* on September 19, 2008, Warner states, "The new paradigm is a way to understand American religion, which is different from European religion. Grace Davie has come along to say that many societies have their own ways of dealing with religion. I think that is terribly important. China also has its own way of dealing with religion ... Fenggang Yang's triple market model is brilliant... I would say his model is a Chinese paradigm." Although constructing a paradigm would be a grandiose work, I cannot accept that honor. I do not agree that what I have theorized is a uniquely Chinese paradigm. In the last section of my article, "The Red, Black and Gray Markets of Religion in China" (2006), I suggested some possible application of the triple-market model to medieval Europe, the former Soviet Union, contemporary Latin America, and other societies. I have made further articulation of this in the last chapter of my book, *Religion in China: Survival and Revival under Communist Rule* (2012), entitled "Oligopoly Dynamics: China and Beyond." In fact, more than half of the countries in the world today maintain some form of oligopoly in their state-religion relations, and the dynamics of religion-state relations in those societies may share many similarities.

In my view, the seeming modesty of Warner's assumption of multiple paradigms for the United States, Europe, and China betrays the nature of science or social science. "If it would be foolish to try to formulate a physics that only applies to the United States, or a biology that held only in Korea, it is equally foolish to settle for a sociology of religion that applies only to Western nations" (Stark and Finke 2004: 3). Of course, physical sciences and social sciences are different because social sciences study human beings who have free will and may choose to be different from the common pattern. If physical sciences try to discover laws that are often based on mathematical models, social sciences can only try to discover law-like patterns based on statistical or probability models. Moreover, some social scientists tend to emphasize the affinity between the social sciences and the humanities, while others tend to emphasize the affinity between the social and the natural sciences. While Steve Warner's approach highlights the differences of religion in various countries and regards them as different paradigms, my approach calls for people's attention to common patterns across borders and boundaries. Certainly, social scientists of religion should recognize and appreciate religious variations among individuals, groups, communities, and societies, but science as a modern enterprise, in my view, is to discover law-like patterns across variations. It is on this very principle, I think, that Peter Berger resorts not to the simultaneous multiple paradigms, but rather to developing a new theory for religion in the modern pluralistic world.

A Normative Theory for Religion in the Modern World

Why does Peter Berger seem to ignore the theoretical constructions within the new paradigm and attempt to develop a new paradigm of his own in this new book? I think the critical question here is: a new paradigm for what? It seems that Peter Berger attempts to construct a new paradigm *for religion* in the modern world, instead of a new paradigm *for the social scientific study of religion* in the modern world. That is, he seems to carry on a normative thinking more than a descriptive study, even though his theorizing is in reference to historical facts and empirical observations.

Berger reasons that because modernization and globalization make it inevitable for there to be increased diversity of religion and increased secular discourse in state affairs, believers of different religions and secularisms have to learn to coexist peacefully and amicably in a modern society. In reality, fundamentalism and relativism are common forms of reaction to the pluralizing phenomena in the modern world. In Peter Berger's eyes:

> Both relativism and fundamentalism are dangerous for individuals and much more so for society. Relativism moves individuals toward moral nihilism, fundamentalism toward fanaticism. Neither is attractive as a way of life, but as long as my nihilistic or fanatical neighbors do not seek to impose their views on me, I can live with them and collaborate in taking out the trash. However, the threat to society is harder to manage. If there is no agreement at all on what is permissible behavior (in Emile Durkheim's phrase, no "collective conscience"), the moral basis and consequently the very existence of a society is put in question. It will lack the solidarity that motivates individuals to make sacrifices for fellow members of the society and ultimately motivates them to risk their lives if the society is attacked. Fundamentalism, even if it is not successful in imposing itself on the entire society (with the abovementioned ensuing costs), will bring about ongoing conflict which, even short of civil war, will undermine social stability (p. 66).

For Peter Berger, while fundamentalism and relativism are dangerous, pluralism is a preferred position. He defines the term: "Pluralism is a social situation in which people with different ethnicities, worldviews, and moralities live together peacefully and interact with each other amicably" (p. 1). In other words, pluralism here describes and prescribes an ideal status of coexistence of multiple religions as well as secularisms. This means not merely coexistence, but coexisting peacefully and amicably. Berger recognizes that the term "pluralism" has a double meaning – as a simple description of social facts and an ideology. Although he intends to use it in the descriptive sense, the above paragraph shows that he actually uses the term more as a normative prescription. Making this clear is not to invalidate his new theorizing. To the contrary, I think the real value of his new theory lies exactly here. Secularization has been a loaded term for many people, but it is one entangled with multiple layers and dimensions. It is difficult to untangle these different dimensions, but distinguishing the dimensions is more than a mere mental exercise; rather, it is necessary for moving forward in the social scientific study of religion.

The secularization of the world is at once a sociological theory for describing and explaining social facts, an ideological theory for making normative changes, and a theoretical paradigm carrying thinking inertia. As a sociological theory, it describes and explains the decline of religious beliefs and/or the declining social significance of religion along with modernization. In the meantime, secularization theory has also served as the theoretical justification for the political ideology of secularization. As a political ideology, the advocates of secularization have mobilized state power, intellectual forces, and other resources to fight against religion or the monopoly of religion in social and political life, i.e., to drive religion out of political, educational, and other public institutions. In addition, both the sociological theory and the political ideology have been fossilized as and reinforced by the theoretical paradigm of secularization. As a theoretical paradigm, it frames macro-, meso-, and micro-level theories that treat religious decline or declining significance as the inevitable norm against which it tries to explain away the so-called exceptional or temporary phenomena of religious persistence in modern societies. As Thomas Kuhn (1962) argues, a paradigm usually carries thinking inertia that requires cumulated empirical evidence and a thinking revolution for a breakthrough. Such a scientific revolution or paradigm shift often takes a long and painful process to accomplish. The breaking down of the secularization paradigm is a recent example of the long and painful process of paradigm shift.

The secularization paradigm in the social scientific study of religion has crumbled and has been replaced by new theories of a new paradigm, as discussed in the previous section, but secularization as a political ideology continues to exert social and political influences as the basis for a social engineering program. It is time for social scientists of religion to recognize that agency-driven intentional secularization is one of the major social movements, and this movement has lasted for several hundred years in Europe, as well as in the United States, particularly in the decades of 1870 to 1920 (Marsden 1994; Smith 2003). And most likely this intentional secularization movement will continue in the coming decades. This social movement needs more descriptive studies by social scientists of religion.

I believe here lies the most valuable contribution of Peter Berger's new theorizing. His effort here is not so much constructing a theory for describing and explaining what has happened, but developing a theory for making the desirable change in the world today. When his theorizing is understood this way, the continuity and discontinuity of his theorizing in the past and the present becomes clear, to me at least. As before, he defines modernity by the measure of secularity in society. This insistence may prompt critics of the secularization paradigm to rail, but it is indeed a great insight about the modern world.

> Every modern society depends on a technological and organizational infrastructure that is necessarily based on a secular discourse. This discourse thus has a privileged position in

public life, even if it is limited (as in the United States) by rigorous legal protections of religious freedom (p. 76).

Historically, this secular discourse was first adopted about four hundred years ago in Europe during the formation process of the modern nation-states and served as a principle to avoid religious wars among the nation-states. Berger's discovery of this has great significance for understanding modernizing societies.

> As I mentioned in the preceding chapter, the most succinct phrase to describe the secular discourse of modernity was coined over four hundred years ago – by Hugo Grotius (1583 – 1645), the Dutch jurist who was one of the founders of international law. Grotius proposed that this law should be formulated in purely secular terms, without any religious assumptions – *etsi Deus non daretur*, "as if God were not given," that is, "as if God did not exist." At the time there were pressing reasons why any law, in order to be internationally accepted, had necessarily to be framed in theologically neutral terms. Western Christendom had been split into two by the Reformation; there were Catholic and Protestant states, and even the Protestant ones adhered to different versions of the Reformation faith – Lutheran, Calvinist, Arminian, Anglican. What is more, if the new law proposed by Grotius was to be truly international, it had to seek adherence from states adhering to Eastern Christian Orthodoxy (notably the rising power of Russia) and to Islam (notably the Ottoman Empire) (pp. 52–53).

The critical importance of this discovery may take an effort to appreciate, especially for religious believers. As it happened, when God was taken out of the discourse of international relations, the ignition of religious wars among the nation-states was deactivated. There have been wars since then, and religion has often played some role, but it was no longer the major ignition. Furthermore, this principle in various manifestations was later taken as a solution for violent conflicts within a nation-state as well. "This was to be the foundation of international law, eventually understood as applying to all state law, based only on reason and what Grotius understood to be natural law separate from revealed religion" (p. 47). It may not be presumptuous to say that such agency-driven intentional secularization has contributed to the diffusion of modernity in various societies and across the world, even though modernity itself is subject to theological and philosophical criticism.

In sum, modernization means to secularize the state and public institutions in order to avoid religious wars and religion-driven social conflicts. When the social history of modernizing Europe is understood this way, it is natural to propose a social engineering program of intentional secularization for the purposes of peace among nation-states and within modernizing society. This normative theory of secularization – agency-driven, intentional differentiation of religion from other social institutions – is indeed what many modern thinkers have advocated and various social reformers have put into practice in many countries.

Further, Peter Berger argues that the particular legal and social arrangements of such agency-driven intentional secularization may be different in different societies. The United Kingdom has maintained a state church where the monarch is the head of the church, even though this has evolved from protecting one particular church in the past into affirming multiple faiths today. The United States was the first country that formally separated church and state through its Constitution, and the First Amendment to the Constitution prevents the state from establishing a religion or prohibiting the free exercise of any religion. France, after many years of struggles against the monopoly of the Roman Catholic Church, eventually settled with *laïcité* in 1905, which forcefully subjects religion (the Roman Catholic Church) to the state and takes it out of education and other public institutions. Although both the US and French models maintain the separation of religion and state, the French model is both anti-clerical and supportive to church institutions through expropriation of church properties, which became supported by state funds, whereas the US model is both encouraging to religion for the purpose of the moral order of society and protecting the freedom of nonconventional religion. In the US model, equal protection of the religious freedom of various religions is inscribed in the First Amendment to the Constitution. The Soviet Union, in Peter Berger's line of theorizing, would be regarded as a modern society as well because of the predominant secular discourse, but it took even harsher measures than France to cleanse religion from society. Adopting Shmuel Eisenstadt's idea of "multiple modernities," Berger affirms all of these various models of modernity. But being modern itself should not be the ultimate goal. We also need to assess the positive and negative consequences of these various models when they are applied to modernizing societies as well as in their original societies.

The Chinese Experiments of Agency-Driven Secularization

What happened in Europe more than four hundred years ago and in the United States more than two hundred years ago might be the result of peculiar historical developments in those societies at the time. However, those happenings have practically defined what is modern in the social and global sense. For late-developing countries, their modernization is not self-initiated but forced upon them as part of and/or a reaction to Western colonialism and imperialism. However, because their modernization was initiated later than in Europe and the United States, their striving for modernization has multiple options in the existing models of religion-state relations. In fact, the Chinese have experimented with various models of agency-driven intentional secularization in their modernization endeavor. Instead of one society maintaining one type of modernity, China has rolled out multiple modernities within one country, sometimes simultaneously.

The Chinese modernization endeavor did not start until the later part of the nineteenth century, not until after several defeats and humiliations by colonialist and imperialist powers of the West, Russia, and Japan. Around the turn of the twentieth century, some literati-turned-modern-intellectuals, such as Kang Youwei (1858–1926), began to advocate for social and political reforms purposely modeled on Western countries and on modernizing Japan. In terms of religion-state relations, Meiji Japan was modeled on Prussia/Germany, with an absolute monarchy based on the state Shinto. At that time, Britain maintained a constitutional monarchy based on the state religion of Anglicanism. Japan and Britain inspired Kang Youwei, who began to advocate for social reforms under the Qing Emperor and for establishing Confucianism as the state religion. Even after the Republican Revolution in 1911 that overthrew the Qing Dynasty, Kang Youwei continued his efforts to re-establish a monarchy based on state Confucianism, either through Yuan Shikai (1859–1916), the Republican president who declared himself the emperor in 1915–16, or through restoring Manchu Emperor Aisin-Gioro Puyi (1906–1967) in 1917. Both of these experiments of a monarchy based on state Confucianism failed. Furthermore, because of the close association between Confucianism and monarchism, Confucianism became the target of the iconoclastic anti-tradition campaigns of the New Culture and May Fourth Movements in the 1910s and 1920s. The modernist intellectuals accused Confucianism of being the spiritual and cultural culprit responsible for China's backwardness, weaknesses, and humiliations by the imperialist powers. The discourses of the Chinese modernist intellectuals very much echoed the French Enlightenment attacks on the Roman Catholic Church.

At the time of the founding of the first republic in Asia, the model of the political institution was the United States. Long before the successful Republican Revolution in 1911, Sun Zhongshan (Sun Yat-sen, 1866–1925) advocated social and political revolutions to overthrow the Qing Dynasty and establish a republic. Before his revolutionary activities, the young Sun Zhongshan was educated in an Episcopal school in Hawaii and was later baptized in a Christian church in Hong Kong. His ideas of a constitutional republic were clearly based on the US model, even though he envisioned five branches instead of three branches of government. At the founding of the Republic of China in 1912, the provisional president, Sun Zhongshan, oversaw the enactment of the Provisional Constitution of the Republic of China, in which Article 7 was about religious freedom for all citizens. Evidently this was modeled on the United States: There is no establishment of a state religion, no religious test for public office, and citizens have the freedom to believe in any religion.

In the early years of the Republic of China, some Chinese intellectuals reacted strongly to the attempts to reestablish a Confucianism-based monarchy, as
advocated by Kang Youwei and his associates. Unlike Sun Zhongshan, however,
these intellectuals consciously adopted the French Enlightenment discourse in
rejecting religion. In 1915, a new magazine, *Xin Qingnian* (New Youth), was
launched. In the inaugural editorial, "A Letter to Youths," the founder, Chen
Duxiu (1878–1942), offered six instructions to Chinese youths: Be free and not
enslaved; be progressive and not conservative; be engaged and not removed;
be global and not parochial; be practical and not rhetorical; be scientific and
not superstitious. Moreover, the new magazine had a French name, *La Jeunesse*,
as well as the Chinese name, *Xin Qingnian*, on the cover. The inaugural issue also
included an article by Chen Duxiu entitled, "The French and the Modern Civilization," which openly called for adopting the French model of modern civilization based on the principles of Liberté, Egalité, and Fraternité. This new magazine became the flagship in promoting progressive values of liberty, equality,
democracy, and science, while rejecting Confucianism. For example, in 1918,
Lu Xun (1881–1936) published his first short story, "A Madman's Diary," in
this magazine; this, together with several other short stories thereafter, served
as scathing indictments of the traditional culture based on Confucianism. He referred to Confucian ethics as cruel and inhumane cannibalism. Meanwhile, Pe-
king University, under the modernist chancellor Cai Yuanpei (1868–1940), who
studied in Germany and France, rallied the campaigners of the new culture, including Chen Duxiu (1879–1942), Li Dazhao (1888–1927), and Hu Shih (1891–
1962), whose Enlightenment thinking heavily influenced the university students
in their participation in the May Fourth Movement of 1919. It seems clear that the
French anti-clerical discourse was adopted in the New Culture and May Fourth
Movements that resolutely rejected Confucianism, then Christianity, then finally
all religions. Until today, the dominant view of Chinese cultural and political
elites is that religion should not meddle in public institutions, which is very
much in a French tone if not in the Soviet pitch.

The New Culture and May Fourth Movements prepared the way for the importation of Marxism-Leninism. In fact, some of the leaders of the New Culture
Movement, such as Chen Duxiu and Li Dazhao, became founders of the Chinese
Communist Party, which was formally established in 1921 under the direct instruction of the Comintern. For the Chinese Communists, the French Enlightenment discourse was supplanted by the Bolshevik ideology of atheism. After the
establishment of the People's Republic of China on the mainland in 1949, the
Chinese Communist Party (CCP) went even further than the Soviet Union.
After making preparations in the 1950s, eventually the CCP tried, from 1966 to

1979, to eradicate religion from the entire society. The only other country that totally banned religion was Albania under Enver Hoxha.

The social philosophies of the Enlightenment and Marxism-Leninism have served as the theoretical justification for the Communist government, in the name of social and political progress, to carry out political campaigns to rid social institutions and the entire society of religion. However, by the end of the twentieth century, it became evident that Communist eradication efforts had all failed. The irreligiousness of the masses under Communist rule was superficial, illusive, or temporary at best (Greeley 1994; Gautier 1997; Froese 2001, 2004a, 2004b). And in most of the post-Communist European societies, following the collapse of the Soviet bloc around 1990, religion rebounded quickly.

Since the early 1980s, the CCP officials and theoreticians of Marxism-Leninism-Maoism (MLM) have repeatedly and sneeringly exclaimed about the "religious fevers" spreading in Chinese society. In their eyes, religious vitality is abnormal in the current social context: China has been undergoing rapid modernization under the leadership of the atheist Communist Party. In such a context, religion logically should decline, as predicted by the Marxist-Leninist secularization theory. Indeed, this even contradicts the secularization theories espoused by non-Marxist social scientists in the West. Peter Berger's *The Sacred Canopy* (1967) and *A Rumor of Angels* (1970) were translated into Chinese and published in China in 1991 and 2003, respectively. During this period of time, many other classic books by authors such as Emile Durkheim, Max Weber, and other Western social scientists and social philosophers were translated into Chinese and published in China for the first time. Although the introduction of various theories of religion was stimulating to Chinese researchers of religion, these newly translated books only contributed to a heightened sense of confusion and bewilderedness among MLM theoreticians and policy-makers—so much so that the former director of the State Administration of Religious Affairs, Ye Xiaowen, sought a private audience with Peter Berger during his first visit to Beijing in 2008. Berger, who might have felt flattered by the attentions of the top CCP official in charge of managing religious affairs, nonetheless went on to reiterate his rescindment of the secularization thesis, as he had been doing since the late 1990s, and he explained the resurgence of religion all around the world.

Elsewhere, I have analyzed the two versions of atheism that have dominated China under Communist rule: Enlightenment atheism and militant atheism.

Enlightenment atheism regards religion as an illusory or false consciousness, being both non-scientific and backward; thus, atheist propaganda is necessary to expunge the misleading religious ideas. In comparison, militant atheism treats religion as the dangerous opium and narcotic of the people, a wrong political ideology serving the interests of the exploiting classes and the antirevolutionary elements; thus, the political forces are necessary to control and eliminate religion (Yang 2012: 46).

Here I would say that in terms of religion-state relations, these correspond to the French and Soviet models, respectively. Both of these models remain strong among Chinese cultural and political elites today, so there is little hope for more relaxation of religious regulations in the near future (Yang 2013).

But in the other line of development of modern Chinese history, the US model of religion-state relations has persisted and flourished. In the first decade of the Republic of China, there were great efforts by political and religious elites to defend the constitutional right of religious freedom and to resist making Confucianism the state religion (Liu 2011). Following several decades of civil wars and the Resistance War against the Japanese Invasion, at the end of 1946, a new Constitution of the Republic of China was passed, which reaffirmed religious freedom in Article 13. Unfortunately, this Constitution was soon suspended in 1948 with the "Temporary Provisions Effective During the Period of Communist Rebellion." In 1949, defeated by the Chinese Communists on the mainland, the Kuomintang-led government withdrew to the island of Taiwan and preserved the Republic of China and its Constitution along with the Temporary Provisions. But not until 1987 was martial law lifted, and not until 1991 were the "Temporary Provisions" abolished. Since then, the Republic of China on Taiwan has become thoroughly democratized, with multiple political parties and direct elections for president and the Congress within the effective boundaries of the Republic of China, which includes Taiwan and some islands off the Chinese mainland. In terms of religion-state relations, the Republic of China on Taiwan has become one of the freest societies in the world today. Thus social and cultural differences do not make a case for exceptionalism.

In the twenty-first century, Chinese intellectuals have started a new round of debates about the strengths and weaknesses of the various models of religion-state relations. At present, the Soviet model remains the arrangement de jure in the political system under Communist rule, and the MLM theoreticians and ideologues show no sign of retreat in their position. In fact, militant atheism has prevailed in recent years, both among rank-and-file cadres in the bureaus of religious affairs and in some corners of the academies of social sciences (Yang 2013).

Meanwhile, amid the revivals of religions and Confucianism, some of the new Confucian leaders in mainland China (*dalu xin rujia*) have refurbished the century-old arguments for making Confucianism the state religion. Not surprisingly, some of these people also express nostalgia for constitutional monarchy, even to the extent of wishing to restore some kind of monarchism. This is anachronistic. Even though the state-church model was prevalent about a hundred years ago among modern or modernizing societies, almost all European countries had de-established the state church by the end of the twentieth century. After World War II, Japan, under the occupation of the US-led Allied Powers, de-established Shinto. The United Kingdom retains the state church de jure, but, as described by Peter Berger, the monarch has declared herself the protector of plural faiths. Nowadays, most of the countries that maintain a state religion are Muslim-dominant or Buddhist-dominant countries that are undergoing painful struggles towards modernization.

In the meantime, many of the liberal intellectuals in mainland China who have abandoned the Soviet discourse and are suspicious of the British model are secularists by default. They either have little to say about religion or would fall back on the French model that once prevailed in the New Culture and May Fourth Movements, i.e., keeping religion out of public institutions. Indeed, many of them regard MLM as a kind of religion that should be secularized.

At present, only a small minority of people in the mainland have openly called for adopting the US model that both prohibits the state establishment of religion and protects the freedom of religion. This minority includes some *weiquan* lawyers who have defended civil and human rights within the framework of the existing legal system, some scholars who have specialized in American studies, and some leaders of Christian house churches. How much will this minority grow in size and influence? This remains to be seen.[1]

Conceptual Clarification for the Descriptive Theory of Religious Pluralism

Peter Berger's new theorizing is a very valuable contribution in laying out various models of religion-state relations, each of which is modern, according to Berger, as long as it attains a certain level of secularity as the dominant discourse in public affairs. Meanwhile, some models are more secular than others, e.g., restricting religion from playing roles in public institutions is more secular than church-state separation. This sheds much light on religion-state relations in

---

1 A new development is worth mentioning here: On May 5 – 7, 2014, a symposium on "Religious Freedom and Chinese Society" was held at Purdue University. The participants, including Chinese lawyers, ministers, and scholars, initiated the "Purdue Consensus on Religious Freedom," which was signed by 52 people and released to the public on May 14, 2014. This Chinese consensus is very much in line with the US model.

the modern world. However, his theorizing stops here, without assessing the social, cultural, and human costs and consequences of the various models. Also, is there any discernable trend of change in the religion-state relations among Western countries, as well as among developing countries? Answering such questions falls within the scope of the descriptive studies of the social scientific study of religion.

For the purpose of description, observation, and explanation of religion-state relations in the world today, it is necessary to make some conceptual clarification. As it stands, Berger's new book has two conceptual confusions. It conflates plurality and pluralism on the one hand, and it conflates individual and social pluralism on the other.

About the first confusion, Berger admits:

> The suffix "ism" [in pluralism] of course suggests an ideology, and for a time I used the more descriptive term "plurality" instead. I then found that I had to keep explaining what I was talking about – "you know, like pluralism." The latter term is readily understood and indeed has become part of ordinary language. I am here using the term in its vernacular meaning (p. 1).

Unfortunately, the vernacular use of pluralism may be a reflection of the inertia of old-paradigm thinking, which conflates the descriptive and normative meanings. Although many scholars continue to use the term pluralism indiscriminately, an increasing number of renowned scholars in the social scientific study of religion have tried to distinguish the descriptive and normative uses. James A. Beckford (1999) suggests using "diversity" for the former and "pluralism" for the latter. Robert Wuthnow substantiates these distinctions succinctly in his 2003 presidential address to the Society for the Scientific Study of Religion: "If diversity is concerned descriptively with the degree of heterogeneity among units within a society, pluralism refers to the normative evaluation of this diversity and with the social arrangements put in place to maintain these normative judgments" (2003: 162).

Following the lead of these scholars, since 2009 I have argued for the adoption of the word "plurality" along with "diversity." In my theorizing, the term plurality describes the *degree* of religious heterogeneity within a society, whereas pluralism refers to the *social arrangement* favorable for a high or relatively higher level of plurality. Obviously, some societies have lower degrees of religious plurality than other societies, and plurality may increase in a given society. Pluralization is the term for the *process* of increasing plurality in a society. For the purpose of theoretical construction, it is helpful, for me at least, to have this set of words with a common root (plu, plur, or plus, which means "more"). The three terms – plurality, pluralism, and pluralization – point to the degree, the arrangement, and the process of plural religions in a society, respectively. The social arrangement of religious pluralism means (1) accepting, affirming, and equally protecting the presence of plural religions in a society; (2) setting up social institutions; (3) creating favorable social and cultural conditions for the presence of plural religions; and (4) granting and protecting for individuals the freedom to choose whatever religion they want, or no religion at all.

According to this definition, pluralism is indeed a normative term. Apparently, Peter Berger's definition ("Pluralism is a social situation in which people with different ethnicities, worldviews, and moralities live together peacefully and interact with each other amicably" [p. 1]) is in the normative sense, rather than describing the simple phenomenon of plural religions coexisting within one society, which is more appropriately called plurality or diversity. As a descriptive variable, plurality can be low or high. High plurality does not necessarily mean that multiple religions coexist within a given society in a peaceful or amicable relationship. For example, multiple religions coexisted along the ancient Silk Road, as mentioned by Peter Berger, but their coexistence may not always have been peaceful and amicable. Rather, there could be violent clashes on a small or large scale. The increase in plurality, i.e., pluralization, may not necessarily lead to pluralism in the sense of people accepting and appreciating each other. In fact, religious conflicts are frequent in many modernizing societies, sometimes in the form of persecution of certain religions, and sometimes in the form of anti-cult measures and campaigns. Modernization takes place along with pluralization, i.e., an increase in the number of religions in a society, but the social and legal arrangement may not be favorable for the peaceful coexistence of plural religions. In other words, high plurality does not necessarily correspond to pluralism in the social and political arrangement. How much accord or discord there is in a society or societies is an empirical question for the social scientific study of religion.

Second, it is necessary to distinguish pluralism at the social and at the individual levels. Peter Berger offers a great insight into the interaction of pluralism at the social and individual levels:

> Pluralism is usually discussed as a social phenomenon, and so it is. However, there is also a pluralism in the mind. As I argued at some length in the preceding chapter, pluralism has the effect of relativizing worldviews by bringing home the fact that the world can be understood differently. In other words, individuals can no longer take for granted the worldview into which they happened to be born (p. 28–29).

But distinction precedes interaction. At the individual level, pluralism is a personal perspective, philosophy, or lifestyle of dealing with multiple religions within one's own mind and heart. It is a philosophical or theological position different from exclusivism, inclusivism, or relativism (see Hemeyer 2009). At the social level, it is a social configuration of dealing with multiple religions within a given society. These two levels are closely related, but they are not the same. As Robert Wuthnow puts it, "A pluralist [person] is someone who can see and appreciate all points of view, a person who is presumably tolerant, informed, cosmopolitan, and a pluralist society is one in which social arrangements favor the expression of diverse perspectives and lifestyles" (Wuthnow 2004: 162–163). Conceptualized in this way, we can see that in a pluralistic society, a person may favor a pluralistic social arrangement without buying into a personal philosophy of pluralism or relativism. Indeed, this is the traditional position of the free churches in modern Europe, the United States, and other parts of the world.

For instance, some evangelicals and fundamentalists in the United States do not hold a pluralistic philosophy in their beliefs. They are exclusivists, believing their religion is the only true religion and all other religions are false. Nonetheless, they would fight for the social arrangement of religious pluralism in which they could hold on to their right of religious freedom without governmental interference. Many of the worries about the fundamentalist takeover or new theocracy have actually resulted from a confusion of individual pluralism with social pluralism. But in the real world, few fundamentalist Christians in the US would give up their religious freedom or try to take away others' religious freedom, which is theologically guaranteed by their perceived God and legally guaranteed by the First Amendment to the Constitution. In other words, Christian evangelicals and fundamentalists may reject theological or philosophical pluralism but will fight for maintaining the social arrangement of religious pluralism. The social scientists of religion must not confuse the individual and the social levels of religious pluralism, even though the two levels may interact with each other and the interaction can be studied as an empirical phenomenon (e.g., Barker 2003).

In short, social pluralism does not require individual pluralism. Legal arrangement and rule of law are the key for peaceful coexistence of plural religions.

Conclusion

In his new book, Peter Berger takes one step back and then tries to waltz forward. First, he articulates two kinds of pluralism [read as plurality]: the coexistence of multiple religions, and the coexistence of religious and secular discourses. Moreover, these two pluralities have to be reflected in people's consciousness; that is, people have to internalize these pluralities in their minds and express them in social behaviors. In a pre-modern society, people may hold a religion as taken for granted, while in a modern society, people have to choose among plural religions as well as secularisms. Indeed, a modern person has to be able to compartmentalize his or her own chosen religion amid many religions and know when to suspend religion and apply a certain secular discourse, such as running a governmental office or piloting an airplane. To achieve pluralism as an ideal state of peaceful and amicable coexistence of plural religions as well as secularisms, Peter Berger offers an agency-driven secularization theory within the new paradigm, which affirms pluralism. This new theory may serve as a theoretical basis for an intentional secularization program of social engineering for a modernizing society. It is a valuable contribution, but it needs conceptual clarification to become a useful conceptual tool for the social scientific study of religion and religious pluralism.

Peter Berger quotes Edward Gibbon: "The common people thought that all religions were equally true, the philosophers that all religions were equally false, the magistrates that all religions were equally useful" (p. 80). I would add to this: The social scientists try to treat all religions equally in search of law-like patterns of change and interactions with other social institutions.

References

Barker, Eileen. 2003. "And the Wisdom to Know the Difference? Freedom, Control and the Sociology of Religion." *Sociology of Religion* 64 no. 3: 285–307.

Beckford, James A. 1999. "The management of religious diversity in England and Wales with special reference to prison chaplaincy." *MOST Journal on Multicultural Societies* 1 (available from: http://unesdoc.unesco.org/images/0014/001437/143733E.pdf#page=19).

Berger, Peter L. 1967. *The Sacred Canopy: Elements of a Sociological Theory of Religion.* New York: Doubleday.

——. 1970. *A Rumor of Angels: Modern Society and the Rediscovery of the Supernatural.* New York: Anchor.

Berger, Peter L., Grace Davie, and Effie Fokas. 2008. *Religious America, Secular Europe? A Theme and Variations.* London: Ashgate Publishing.

Casanova, José. 1994. *Public Religions in the Modern World.* Chicago: University of Chicago Press.

Davie, Grace. 1994. *Religion in Britain since 1945: Believing Without Belonging.* Oxford: Wiley-Blackwell.

——. 2000. *Religion in Modern Europe: A Memory Mutates.* New York: Oxford University Press.

——. 2007. *The Sociology of Religion.* London: Sage.

Fan, Lizhu. 2011. "The Dilemma of Chinese Religious Studies in the Framework of Western Religious Theories." In *Social Scientific Studies of Religion in China: Methodology, Theories, and Findings*, edited by Fenggang Yang and Graeme Lang, 87–108. Leiden and Boston: Brill.

Froese, Paul. 2001. "Hungary for Religion: A Supply-Side Interpretation of the Hungarian Religious Revival." *Journal for the Scientific Study of Religion* 40: 251–268.

——. 2004a. "After Atheism: An Analysis of Religious Monopolies in the Post-Communist World." *Sociology of Religion* 65: 57–75.

——. 2004b. "Forced Secularization in Soviet Russia: Why an Atheistic Monopoly Failed." *Journal for the Scientific Study of Religion* 43: 35–50.

Gautier, Mary L. 1997. "Church Attendance and Religious Belief in Postcommunist Societies." *Journal for the Scientific Study of Religion* 36: 289–97.

Greeley, Andrew. 1994. "A Religious Revival in Russia?" *Journal for the Scientific Study of Religion* 33: 253–72.

Hamberg, Eva M. and Thorleif Pettersson. 1994. "The Religious Market: Denominational Competition and Religious Participation in Contemporary Sweden." *Journal for the Social Scientific Study of Religion* 33: 205–216.

Hemeyer, Julia Corbett. 2009. *Religion in America (6th Edition)*. New York: Pearson.

Kuhn, Thomas S. 1962. *The Structure of Scientific Revolution*. Chicago: University of Chicago Press.

Liu, Yi. 2012. "Confucianism, Christianity, and Religious Freedom: Debates in the Transformation Period of Modern China (1900–1920s)." In *Confucianism and Spiritual Traditions in Modern China and Beyond*, edited by Fenggang Yang and Joseph Tamney. 247–276. Leiden and Boston: Brill.

Marsden, George M. 1994. *The Soul of the American University: From Protestant Establishment to Established Nonbelief*. New York: Oxford University Press.

Smith, Christian. 1998. *American Evangelicalism: Embattled and Thriving*. Chicago: University of Chicago Press.

——. 2003. *The Secular Revolution: Power, Interests, and Conflict in the Secularization of American Public Life*. Berkeley and Los Angeles, Cal.: University of California Press.

Stark, Rodney and Laurence R. Iannaccone. 1994. "A Supply-Side Reinterpretation of the 'Secularization' of Europe." *Journal of the Scientific Study of Religion* 33: 230–252.

Stark, Rodney and Roger Finke. 2000. *Acts of Faith: Explaining the Human Side of Religion*. Berkeley, Cal.: University of California Press.

——. 2004. "To the Chinese Readers," *Xinyang de Faze (Acts of Faith)*, translated by Fenggang Yang. Beijing: Renmin University Press.

Warner, R. Stephen. 1993. "Work in Progress Toward a New Paradigm for the Sociological Study of Religion in the United States." *American Journal of Sociology* 98: 1044–1093.

——. 2002. "More Progress on the New Paradigm." In *Sacred Markets, Sacred Canopies: Essays on Religious Markets and Religious Pluralism*, edited by Ted G. Jelen, 1–32. Lanham, Md.: Rowman & Littlefield Publishers.

Wuthnow, Robert. 2004. "Presidential Address 2003: The Challenge of Diversity." *Journal for the Scientific Study of Religion* 43: 159–70, 162.

Yang, Fenggang. 2006. "The Red, Black, and Gray Markets of Religion in China." *Sociological Quarterly* 47: 93–122.

——. 2012. *Religion in China: Survival and Revival under Communist Rule*. New York: Oxford University Press.

——. 2013. "A Research Agenda on Religious Freedom in China." *The Review of Faith and International Affairs* 11 no. 2: 6–17.

Index